micro
living

micro living

40 INNOVATIVE TINY HOUSES EQUIPPED FOR FULL-TIME LIVING, IN 400 SQUARE FEET OR LESS

DEREK "DEEK" DIEDRICKSEN

Storey Publishing

The mission of Storey Publishing is to serve our customers by publishing practical information that encourages personal independence in harmony with the environment.

EDITED BY Hannah Fries and Michal Lumsden
TECHNICAL EDIT BY Phil Schmidt
ART DIRECTION AND BOOK DESIGN BY Carolyn Eckert
TEXT PRODUCTION BY Erin Dawson

COVER PHOTOGRAPHY BY Getaway, photos by Bearwalk, spine (bottom); Craft & Folk Art Museum, Los Angeles, CA, front (bottom right); © Derek Diedricksen, front (bottom center), spine (top), back (bottom left & author), inside front; Designed by David Latimer, photos by StudioBuell, front (top & bottom left); Dustin Diedricksen, inside back; Kasita, spine (middle); TinyHouseBasics.com, back (top left & right)

INTERIOR PHOTOGRAPHY BY © Derek Diedricksen, except: Andrew M. Odom, Tiny r(E)volution, Cofounder, 59; Courtesy of Brenda Kelly, 121; Brian Burk, 141; © Christopher Tack, 1, 68 top left & middle right, 70 top; Craft & Folk Art Museum, Los Angeles, CA, 3, 9 bottom and 232–234; Darin J. Zaruba, 146–150; Designed by David Latimer, photos by StudioBuell, 2 top, 78–83; Gary Kufner Studio/Athens GA, 94 top; Getaway, photos by Bearwalk, 10 bottom and 122–125; Hayden Spurdle, 118–120; © ideabug/iStock.com, 176 right, 179 top left; JamaicaCottageShop.com, 40–43; Jewel D. Pearson, Ms. Gypsy Soul Tiny House Project, 126–131; Kasita, 6 and 44–49; Kyle Woolard, 142 top, 144 bottom; Mike Bedsole/ Tiny House Chattanooga, 28–33; MJ Boyle/Tiny House Designer, Builder & Occupant, 132–139; Rocky Mountain Tiny Houses, 10 top, 226–231; © Robinson Residential Design, 98–100; courtesy of Ryan Nicodemus, 167; Sally Cooper Photography, 142 bottom, 144 top, 145; © Samuel Laubscher, 84 bottom left; TinyHouseBasics. com, 5 and 50–55; Tumbleweed Tiny House Company, 106, 108–111; Vera Struck 198–201; © Zane S. Spang, 11 top right and 208–211

ILLUSTRATIONS BY © Phil Hackett
PLAN DRAWINGS BY Ilona Sherratt, except CAFAM drawings by Sean Carey

© 2018 BY DEREK DIEDRICKSEN

STOREY BOOKS ARE AVAILABLE at special discounts when purchased in bulk for premiums and sales promotions as well as for fund-raising or educational use. Special editions or book excerpts can also be created to specification. For details, please call 800-827-8673, or send an email to sales@storey.com.

STOREY PUBLISHING
210 MASS MoCA Way
North Adams, MA 01247
storey.com

Printed in Hong Kong by Printplus Ltd.
10 9 8 7 6 5 4 3

Library of Congress Cataloging-in-Publication Data

Names: Diedricksen, Derek, author.
Title: Micro living : 40 innovative tiny houses equipped for full-time living, in 400 square feet or less / by Derek "Deek" Diedricksen.
Description: North Adams, MA : Storey Publishing, 2018.
Identifiers: LCCN 2018012692 (print)
  | LCCN 2018013508 (ebook)
  | ISBN 9781612128771 (ebook)
  | ISBN 9781612128764 (pbk. : alk. paper)
Subjects: LCSH: Small houses. | Domestic space.
Classification: LCC NA7533 (ebook)
  | LCC NA7533 .D54 2018 (print)
  | DDC 728—dc23
LC record available at
  https://lccn.loc.gov/2018012692

CONTENTS

SO I SUPPOSE IT'S AN ADDICTION gone right — an obsession, at least, that's not too detrimental to my health. Then again, it's all in how you look at it. Right now, as I type this, I'm aboard a flight returning from Reykjavik, Iceland, with an Iron Maiden shirt stuffed behind my back to stifle my chronic building-related back pain. But I can't complain: I was just in Iceland, looking for hidden urban tree houses while digging for daring and funky design ideas.

The obsession I'm talking about is tiny houses — designing them and building them. While my last book, *Microshelters*, included all manner of small structures, this time around we're focusing mainly (with a couple of exceptions) on the "true tinies," as some call them. Not so much forts, tree houses, day-use hobby huts, or bizarre shelters, but bona fide tiny houses. Nonetheless, you'll find an eclectic mix here, and perhaps some will be right up your alley.

I'm not here to judge, although (open mouth, insert foot) you'll see that I have tacked on a "Deek's Takeaways" section for each featured structure. Here I'll offer some words of praise, and possibly some constructive criticism, for the home at hand. As I've told my workshop students, there is much to learn from each and every design, from the good, the bad, and even the incredibly ugly. In addition, I've asked the builder of each tiny home to honestly divulge what, in retrospect, they'd do differently. Some might come off as more honest than others, but many a brave soul has dropped you little tidbits of insight about things that really didn't work out in the long run.

Whether you're leafing through this collection in a bookstore, or settling in for a long read by the light of a fire with a good snifter of who-knows-what, or casually flipping through it on your . . . er . . . throne, I hope you will find ideas and inspiration on these pages. Perhaps you'll pick up a random time- and money-saving method, or maybe you're new to this stuff and will see something that totally changes your world. Heck, this could be your first crack at tiny houses, so I hope you pull something positive from it, whether you intend

to try out this lifestyle or just find the notion absolutely absurd yet worth a curious peek.

But wait, there's more! If you do feel inclined to take a crack at a bare-bones tiny structure (one that you could customize and outfit to serve your own needs), flip to the back of the book, where you'll find construction drawings for just such a structure.

Finally, I'd like to state my opinion that tiny living is not for everyone, and I never push the idea. In fact, you can read Andrew Odom's story (on page 56) about how he came to the same conclusion. You might ask, "Deek, why are you sabotaging the magic and romance of the scene?" I'm not; I'm just being honest. After all, the point here is more about

striving toward simplicity than "going small." My hope is that the idea of scaling back, even just a bit, might turn out to be something you actually want to do, whether you end up with a real tiny house or not.

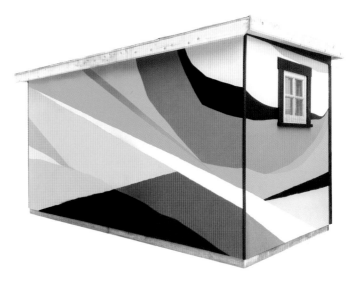

But What Makes a Tiny House "Tiny"?

Go into any tiny house Facebook group or any discussion forum, or even just talk to *anyone* about tiny houses, and I guarantee this will be one of the first questions you're asked (besides where you go to the bathroom) — and rightfully so. See, we as people just love to classify and categorize. This isn't all bad, as it does help to clear things up. So let

me quickly summarize what I mean when I talk about tiny houses. It's pretty darn simple.

For the sake of this collection, my personal standards (with a handful of exceptions) are as follows:

1. **THE DWELLING HAS TO BE FOR FULL-TIME USE**, or at least have the **potential** for it. A few structures in this book are borderline, depending on the climate, or because they lack some amenities, but who's counting? They were too cool and original to leave out. Other featured builds might be rentals or seasonal cabins but have the potential to become full-time homes. Don't cover your eyes and plug your ears because one particular cabin might not have insulation or perhaps a shower worthy of the Ritz Carlton. Look beyond to what else it might offer for inspiration.

2. **I'LL JUST COME OUT AND SAY IT: POOP.** There has to be a way for it to go somewhere. Granted, much of the world still uses outhouses, but we'll stick mainly to indoor bathrooms that are part of the home's design. That said, there are some exceptions in which the solution sits in a separate unit from the home or cabin, or where a bathroom could simply be added to the existing space. In addition, a

space to bathe is another facet most people require in a bathroom, and most of these structures have it.

3. IT'S GOTTA BE SMALL. The maximum square footage of a "tiny" house is often (and sometimes annoyingly) debated, but for the most part we're going with 400 square feet and under. I don't feel that this is the end-all definition, but 400 square feet is indeed tiny.

4. USABLE, COMFORTABLE SLEEPING SPACE IS A MUST. I would have loved to include more of the mind-blowing sheds, backyard studios, forts, tree houses, and writing retreats that I've toured, seen, built, or photographed, but we already hit upon those in *Microshelters*, so the new ones I've discovered since will have to wait until another time.

5. IT SHOULD HAVE SOME KIND OF KITCHEN. Sure, many homes around the world (especially in hotter climates) have kitchens in structures that are separate from the home, but for this book I was looking for homes with kitchens that were part and parcel of the design. I stretched this one a hair for a few structures that offered so much to enjoy, inspire, or learn from that I couldn't leave them out.

6. AND IT NEEDS MEANS FOR HEATING/COOLING (depending on the local climate). Burrito-derived methane doesn't count.

7. SOMETIMES I BREAK MY OWN RULES. But if I chose to include it, it has some interesting design approach, look, creative use of materials, or budget strategy that I thought was worth highlighting.

I've traveled all around the United States and beyond to feature what you're about to see. The houses and shelters I've picked are ones that I found particularly inspiring, innovative, unique, fun, or just plain beautiful. There are about a hundred more I would have liked to feature, but I ultimately feared lawsuits for the back pain caused by lugging around such an enormous book. So 40 it is. Enjoy, and may you drink deeply from the well of photos, stories, ideas, mistakes, and triumphs of others that lies in your hands.

— Derek "Deek" Diedricksen

The Luna Loft

FLINTSTONE, GEORGIA

DESIGN:
Hannah & Enoch Elwell,
Andrew Alms,
Jason Ennis
(Cogent Studio), and
Charles Greenwood
(Greenwood Engineering)

I **PRESENT TO YOU THE TREETOP RENTAL DWELLING** of designers Andrew Alms and Enoch Elwell. This full-fledged tiny house is also one of the more impressive tree houses you may ever lay eyes on. Their design was inspired by the Living Building Challenge, which requires a building to be zero-impact in terms of water and net-positive in energy production. The Alms/Elwell team wasn't able to build the house to meet all the specifications, but it's a goal they aspire to.

The pair made stylish use of reclaimed materials. From the 1860s barn siding and the mesmerizingly cool front door to the enormous support beams salvaged from an old schoolhouse and the array of reused factory windows, this build is full of nods to the past and stories of what was. My brother, Dustin, and I, along with our friend Steven Harrell, spent two nights here on a road trip through nearby Tennessee, and it just wasn't enough time.

While some might think that staying in a tree house would be a childish affair devoid of the real needs of everyday life, this couldn't be further from the truth. The Luna Loft is not only heated and well insulated (with SIPs, structural insulated panels), it also has a full bathroom (with composting toilet), a lounging area with a couch, a fridge, a kitchenette, and a beautiful open loft with a queen-size bed.

Inspiration: "Childhood memories and the potential to play in the trees again. We looked at many tree houses in preparation and ended up basing it off the Hama Hama design by Pete Nelson — but a little wider, higher, and in a two-tree system."

Pennies and foreign coins make for intricate and interesting tile work in the bathroom, and a whiskey-barrel shower stall adds a bit of ingenious whimsy.

These salvaged factory windows are 17 feet tall!

DEEK'S TAKEAWAYS

There's a lot to see in the Luna Loft and plenty of ideas to glean from it. I love the use of thick mesh panels (or "hog panels") for safety railings on the 90-square-foot deck (which is perched 17 feet above the ground). The interior wall paneling is reclaimed 2×6s (which admittedly run the risk of being overly heavy for a tree house). Their diagonal orientation is pleasing to the eye, and this age-old barn-bracing and cladding technique also provides additional strength and rigidity to the structure.

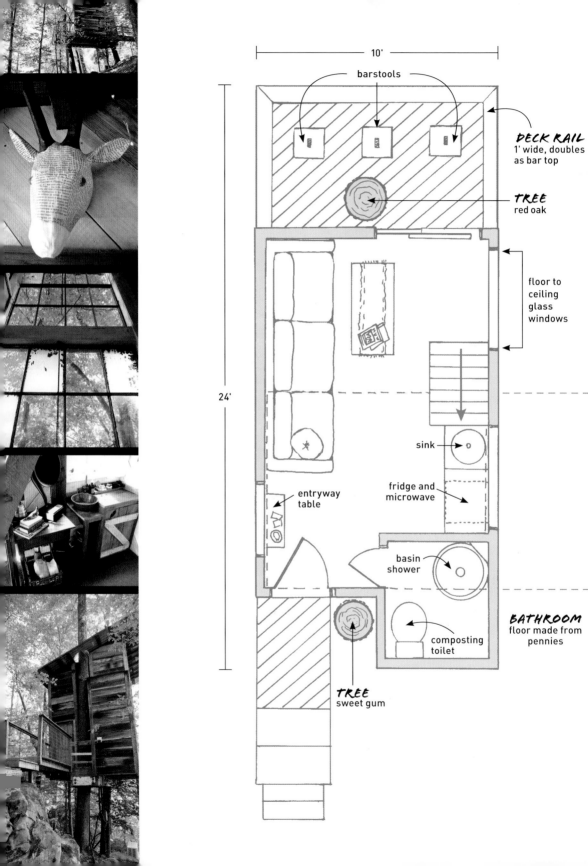

barstools

10'

24'

DECK RAIL
1' wide, doubles
as bar top

TREE
red oak

floor to
ceiling
glass
windows

sink

fridge and
microwave

entryway
table

basin
shower

composting
toilet

BATHROOM
floor made from
pennies

TREE
sweet gum

IN RETROSPECT:

"I wish we had started earlier. It's not that people don't help you or that they mean to hinder you, but inevitably, things like engineering take more time than you have planned. Put an extra 20 percent on your timeline and an extra 30 percent on your cost estimates."

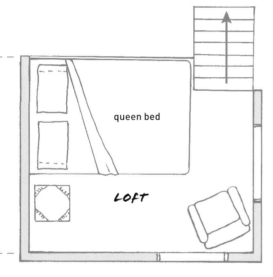

queen bed

LOFT

NOTE:
Dotted line signifies the outline of the loft

THE LUNA LOFT STATS

DIMENSIONS: 24' long × 10' wide × 17' tall (at its peak)

SQUARE FOOTAGE: Main area: 250; loft: 100

BUDGET: Approximately $75,000 (including $34,000 via Kickstarter, $15,000 worth of sponsored materials, and $10,000 from corporate sponsors)

HEATING/COOLING: 15,000 Btu Mitsubishi mini split

BATHROOM: Sun-Mar composting toilet; shower

POWER: Grid-tied (buried from street to site)

HOT WATER: 25-gallon mini tank-style electric water heater

This gorgeous Gothic church window brings interest, color, and light to the room.

Victoria's Salvage Haven

ARGYLE, NEW YORK

DESIGN:
Victoria Cantwell
and friends

ON A RECENT TINY-HOUSE-HUNTING TRIP, I found myself on a last-minute jaunt with my kids to the quaint little town of Argyle, New York, to stay in a charming and rustic tree house. We had needed little convincing to pack our bags and hit the road with our fishing poles, s'mores ingredients, and bug spray. What I didn't know then was that the tree house would end up taking a backseat to another one of the three structures that Vicky rents on her 5-acre organic homestead. On top of that, I was about to discover Vicky's love for roadside salvage and all things odd, vintage, and downright fabulous. Which brings me to what I've dubbed "Victoria's Salvage Haven."

The Haven is a tiny house that was not professionally built or even built with a definite plan. It was built with materials from a shed that previously stood on the same site and clearly adorned with an afterthought or two (or ten). Nothing seems to be what I call KCT (kitchen cabinet tight). But that's the absolute charm of the place! From the worn floorboards to the salvage finds oozing with character (the Gothic church window, for one), it all makes for a very relaxing, scaled-back, no-frills retreat where I instantly felt at ease.

Inspiration: "I am inspired by my love of collecting unique salvaged pieces as well as antique/vintage finds, and creating spaces that blend in with the beauty of the natural surroundings. I love to recycle and bring new life and purpose to what others have thrown away. I wanted to create a place where guests can quiet their minds and experience life unplugged in a quaint, small space that feeds the soul."

What this cabin lacks in square footage is made up for with the extended lines of sight provided by large windows all around. And the addition of a few skylights means you'll never feel close to cramped. As for the decor, it complements and enhances the space — an art not easily mastered. Make no mistake, decor (and finding it cheaply) is a huge part of tiny house building. After all, what makes a cozy dwelling if not the perfect balance of space, light, and color?

The fact that the bathroom is an attached outhouse (not accessible from inside the cabin) means that many in the tiny house scene will refuse to call it a real "tiny house," but these arrangements do work for many people. Yes, the outhouse would be cold in the winter, but it could be insulated, and a slight alteration would make it accessible from the inside. The outdoor cook space, accessed through a back door, is also unconventional, yet it's what I loved most about Victoria's haven. Perhaps staying here could be considered "tiny-house-ish glamping." I really don't care, though, because it's a gorgeous space loaded with tiny hidden details. Don't let the outhouse scare you.

IN RETROSPECT: "I do regret completely leveling the original shed structure. There is a slight slope to the site, too, and that made for a few challenges when installing windows, doors, and floorboards. A more solid base would have been ideal. I would also have put in some floor insulation — that's probably my biggest regret."

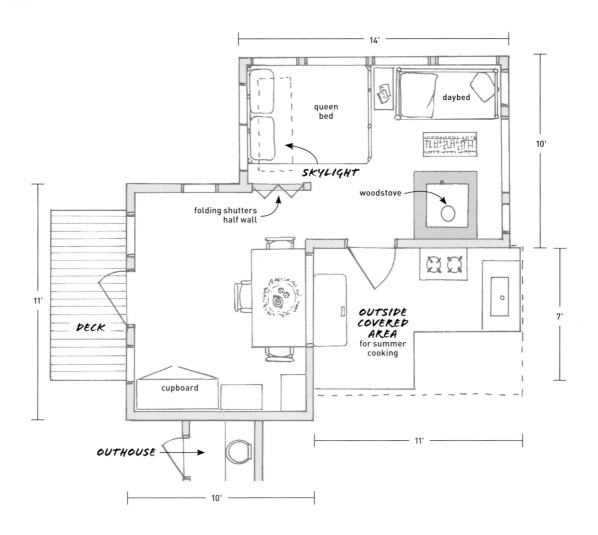

14'

queen bed

daybed

10'

SKYLIGHT

folding shutters half wall

woodstove

11'

DECK

OUTSIDE COVERED AREA
for summer cooking

7'

cupboard

OUTHOUSE

11'

10'

VICTORIA'S SALVAGE HAVEN STATS

DIMENSIONS: First section: 10' long × 11' wide × 7½–9' feet tall (sloped ceiling); second section: 14' long × 10' wide × 6½–8' feet tall (sloped ceiling); overall dimensions: approximately 20' long × 15' wide, including outdoor kitchen and attached outhouse

SQUARE FOOTAGE: 340

BUDGET: $7,000

HEATING/COOLING: Woodstove in winter, many open windows in summer

BATHROOM: Attached outhouse

POWER: Buried electrical service to a breaker box

HOT WATER: Water stored in a 5-gallon vintage water cooler and heated on a stove (a three-burner, vintage, repurposed RV propane cooktop)

Inspiration:
"Freedom from land, and the ability to roam."

The Quarky Turnip Houseboat

SEATTLE, WASHINGTON

DESIGN:
Original builder/
designer unknown

WHILE ON A SPEAKING TOUR for my book *Microshelters*, I stayed in almost a dozen tiny houses — a different one each night of the trip. All were pretty amazing, but I was blown away by the craft and class of the Quarky Turnip, a relatively luxurious houseboat bobbing on the surface of Seattle's Lake Union. Add the fact that it had city views and was docked next to other great houseboats and you have the makings of something truly memorable.

While there are downsides of urban houseboat living — namely, exorbitant docking fees and, well, the possibility of motion sickness — there are quite a few pros, including their mobility. What I love about the Quarky Turnip is not only its color scheme and rounded windows and doorways (reminiscent of gypsy wagons), but also its open layout. The little deck is great, as is the rooftop lounge. When constructing such small dwellings, it really is important to think about each plane, surface, and cubic foot. Ask yourself, "How can I maximize this space, and when and where should I just leave it alone?"

Pit shower

The view from the back deck

One rule of thumb for floating homes is to make the height of your cabin no higher than the berth (width) of your vessel. Otherwise, you could end up with a tippy, unsafe structure. Because of this guideline, narrow — and correspondingly short — houseboats result in less headroom, so for taller people (or, in some cases, most anyone) these boats can be "head slammers." The canal-boat-style floating homes (long and narrow) often have inward-slanted walls to help compensate for this problem, focusing the weight toward the middle. The downsides of this design are that, as with A-frames, there's less room to maneuver side to side, and most furniture, which is designed for vertical walls, doesn't fit well. Also, remember that in a floating home, you have to secure just about everything because your house bobs up and down with the wakes of passing boats, the current, and changing tides.

The only thing about the Quarky Turnip that didn't impress me was the "pit shower" sunk into the bedroom floor, which offered little privacy and made things a bit wet. Showering without walls a mere 12 inches from the side of one's bed, while surrounded by uncovered windows, is a bit of an odd experience. I was able to get clean, though, while waving at the passing neighbors in my birthday suit.

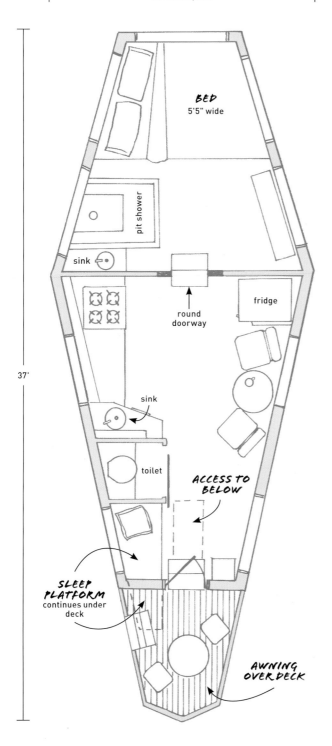

12' widest point

BED
5'5" wide

pit shower

sink

round
doorway

fridge

sink

toilet

*ACCESS TO
BELOW*

37'

*SLEEP
PLATFORM*
continues under
deck

*AWNING
OVER DECK*

IN RETROSPECT:

"Houseboats, while the romantic dream of many, can be very expensive to moor and maintain. Furnishing such uniquely shaped (and moving) structures requires a little patience as well."

THE QUARKY TURNIP HOUSEBOAT STATS

DIMENSIONS: 37' long × 12' wide × 7'6" tall

SQUARE FOOTAGE: 346

BUDGET: Original cost to build unknown

HEATING/COOLING: Electric radiant wall heaters

BATHROOM: Standard flush toilet to central marina septic; pit shower in bedroom

POWER: Hookup from the mainland marina to a breaker panel

HOT WATER: Electric tankless water heater

Bedsole's Lookout

CLEVELAND, TENNESSEE

DESIGN:
Mike Bedsole

EASILY AMONG THE HIGHEST-END of the houses in our collection (up there with the Engberg Tiny House, page 51, and the Alpha Tiny House, page 79), Bedsole's Lookout is the work of Mike Bedsole and his crew from Tiny House Chattanooga. Specializing in elegant simplicity, Mike has been a force in the tiny house scene for several years, and the Lookout showcases why. This particular model broke out at the 2016 Tiny House Jamboree in Colorado Springs and grabbed the people's choice award as "Best in Show" out of nearly 60 houses. Step inside, and right away you get a feeling of spaciousness — and isn't that the point? While cost wasn't much of a concern to the builders, obtrusive lofts were.

No stone is left unturned here. Just consider the open kitchen by the entrance with its flip-up bar, gas range, three-quarter-height fridge, ample sink, butcher block countertops, and washer-dryer space. And other elements, such as the patterned hickory-wood wall in the raised living room and the sliding bathroom door with its attractive hardware, prove that this house takes itself seriously.

Inspiration: "I wanted to build a unit that was geared toward being easy to live in, with a non-laddered loft design for those who don't want to crawl up. I kept it simple enough so that you could just move right in, and it would work. The goal was a simple but functional sleeping area, plenty of storage, and to keep it lavish yet simple."

The loft above the bathroom comes in two configurations, one with space for a bed (but less headroom), the other with storage space sort of like a walk-in closet.

DEEK'S TAKEAWAYS

Many small dwellings sacrifice their high interior space by installing sleep and storage lofts that enclose almost the entire ceiling. The Bedsole Lookout demonstrates a different approach: the master bedroom (which fits a queen bed) is built over the raised, cantilevered end of the gooseneck trailer, leaving 5 feet, 11 inches of headroom, compared to the usual 4 feet or less you find in most loft bedrooms. This very open loft is accessed by stairs instead of a ladder. The stairway and short "hall" to this space conceal a hatch to a very large storage locker beneath. Add to that a rather huge built-in storage shed accessed from outside, and you start to see how much stow-space a tiny house can have, if you get clever.

I really appreciate the multitude of windows (hence the house's name) and the sizable skylight that opens like a bulkhead hatch above the master sleep area. With just a small stepladder, the roof can be accessed easily for repairs, solar-panel cleaning, or even stargazing.

The one-of-a-kind bathroom, both spacious and gorgeous by tiny house standards, contains a full-size shower lined with tiger wood over a Galvalume backer.

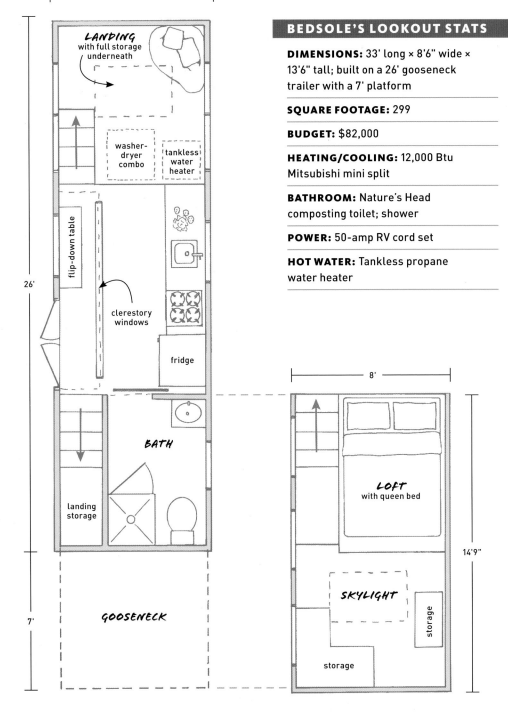

LANDING
with full storage
underneath

washer-
dryer
combo

tankless
water
heater

flip-down table

clerestory
windows

fridge

BATH

landing
storage

GOOSENECK

26'

7'

8'6"

BEDSOLE'S LOOKOUT STATS

DIMENSIONS: 33' long × 8'6" wide × 13'6" tall; built on a 26' gooseneck trailer with a 7' platform

SQUARE FOOTAGE: 299

BUDGET: $82,000

HEATING/COOLING: 12,000 Btu Mitsubishi mini split

BATHROOM: Nature's Head composting toilet; shower

POWER: 50-amp RV cord set

HOT WATER: Tankless propane water heater

LOFT
with queen bed

SKYLIGHT

storage

storage

8'

14'9"

This hickory-wood wall is its own work of art.

IN RETROSPECT:

"In future models we're going to drop the gooseneck another 10 inches, a custom job, which will then give the master bed area a standing height of 6 feet, 9 inches on its high end. Also, I would move the washer-dryer combo into the bedroom area so that dirty clothes don't have to travel across the house, small as it is, to be laundered."

The Willow Tree House

WILLOW, NEW YORK

DESIGN:
Antony Gibbon Designs (UK)

Y ES, THE WILLOW TREE HOUSE, a rental getaway owned by tech-whiz Avner Ronen, breaks our square-footage rule, being close to two times the size of many of the structures we've included. But it's just so kick-butt and unique, I couldn't *not* showcase it. "Small" is relative anyway, and the Willow Tree House is still leagues smaller than the average American home, so here it is in all its glory.

Avner, being equally enthralled with tree houses and tiny houses, admits that the Willow is a twist on both. While not actually built within trees, it still commands a lofty view and almost seems to float above its lighted lower deck (in reality it's held up by its pedestal entrance and two large metal posts). This backwoods escape has a great deck view of a man-made pond below, where you might catch a glimpse of a deer drinking from its shallows. Better yet, you get the same view from the couch through the enormous window a flight above. As if that's not magical enough, the open-air loft not only provides useful space up in the heights of this cabin but also directs its view into the same wilderness beyond. The high ceiling, and the incorporation of windows and skylights, makes this relatively small space seem almost like a cathedral in the woods.

This bedroom for the kids could also be a great office or writing room.

What I love about this place is that regardless of whether you call it a cabin, a tiny house, or a woodland escape, it has everything you need for comfortable and efficient full-time living: a kitchen, bathroom, lounging space, and even luxuries like an outdoor wood-fired hot tub. Its positioning is perfect too, taking in shade and sun during different times of the day and to differing degrees throughout the seasons.

There is also space for the kids (accessed via a hallway leading to the other end of the cabin), where a smaller but still impressive window peers in the other direction into Ronen's 25-acre spread. Meanwhile, the deck below is protected from the rain but without sacrificing the view.

My only critique on this place: There really isn't any storage for goods, or even groceries. In fairness, though, it was designed for short-term stays.

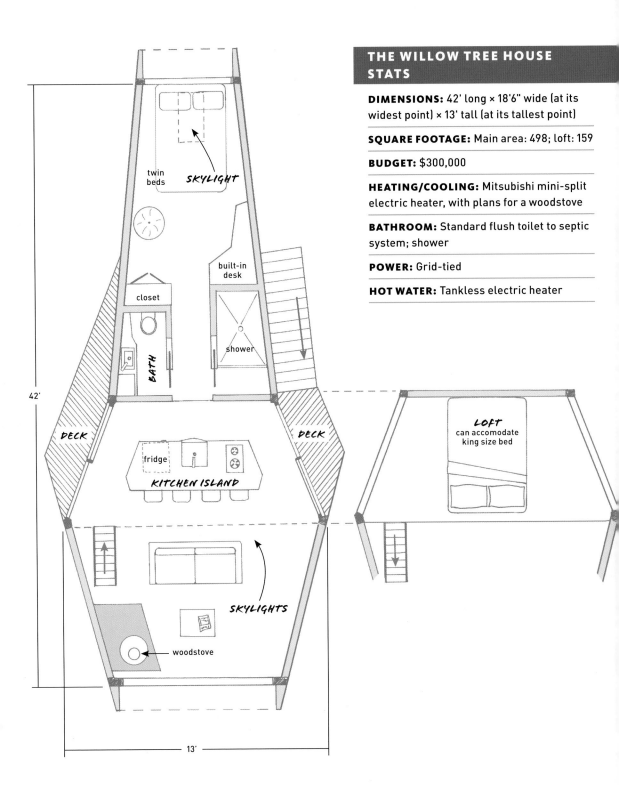

twin
beds

SKYLIGHT

built-in
desk

closet

BATH

shower

DECK

DECK

fridge

KITCHEN ISLAND

SKYLIGHTS

woodstove

LOFT
can accomodate
king size bed

42'

13'

THE WILLOW TREE HOUSE STATS

DIMENSIONS: 42' long × 18'6" wide (at its widest point) × 13' tall (at its tallest point)

SQUARE FOOTAGE: Main area: 498; loft: 159

BUDGET: $300,000

HEATING/COOLING: Mitsubishi mini-split electric heater, with plans for a woodstove

BATHROOM: Standard flush toilet to septic system; shower

POWER: Grid-tied

HOT WATER: Tankless electric heater

IN RETROSPECT: "I wish it had a retractable showerhead, which would have made cleaning easier. I also would have made the porch a bit bigger so that it could fit two chairs and a table for a nice breakfast. More headroom in the loft would be a good idea, too, if I did things over."

The Apple Blossom Cottage

JAMAICA, VERMONT

DESIGN:
Domenic Mangano,
President/Senior Designer,
Jamaica Cottage Shop, Inc.

WELCOME TO THE 802. In Vermont, it's a whole different ballgame in building, from the region's rough terrain to its harsh winters. The Apple Blossom Cottage from Vermont's Jamaica Cottage Shop is more proof that a tiny house doesn't have to be on wheels. This 13 × 26-foot cabin kit has been a huge fan favorite in the Domenic Mangano line for some time and not only comes in kit form or as a plan set but can also be delivered, turnkey, within New England. Dom is no new jack to the game, either. The Jamaica Cottage Shop has been around for well over 20 years and has cranked out thousands of high-quality sheds, garages, tiny houses, and backwoods cabins.

In addition to the usual requirements of comfort and utility, tiny houses here have to take into account that Vermont is, well, cold as all get out. Spray foam insulation is a key ingredient not only in the envelope of the living space but also within shed add-ons where all the electricity and water come in. Neglect to protect your water up here and you're in for a world of expensive problems.

This cottage has all the comforts of home: a spacious 5 × 8-foot bathroom, an open-plan living room with a kitchenette, a separate bunkroom, two storage closets, plenty of standard-size windows, a 4-foot porch with steel balusters, and even a "transforming table" that effortlessly raises from "coffee" to "dining" height.

IN RETROSPECT:

"I would have switched the location of the toilet and the sink to make the bathroom space easier to use and navigate. Some of these things aren't realized until you've lived with a space for a while."

DEEK'S TAKEAWAYS

It's always a tough call: to porch or not to porch? While the answer can be somewhat clearer on wheeled builds ("Why waste the trailer space?" some ask), it's still a matter of looks versus function. I'll admit, while the porch does eat up some square footage on this house, it adds a ton in terms of making the home less boxy, more inviting, and more connected to the outdoors. Sure, you could later add a deck or separate floating porch next to a build, but it wouldn't have the cohesive look that this one has.

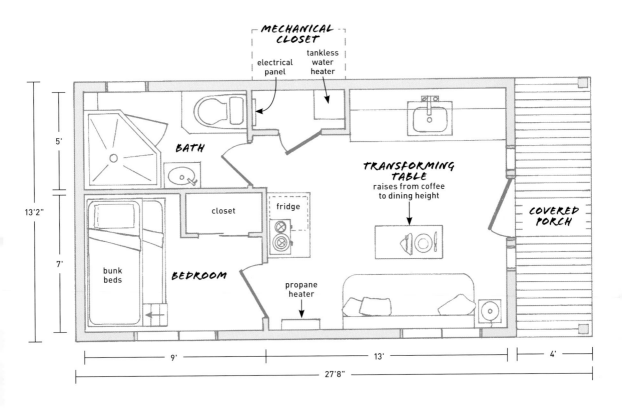

MECHANICAL CLOSET

electrical panel

tankless water heater

BATH

TRANSFORMING TABLE
raises from coffee to dining height

COVERED PORCH

closet

fridge

bunk beds

BEDROOM

propane heater

5'

13'2"

7'

9'

13'

4'

27'8"

The open-plan living room and kitchenette is both roomy and cozy.

THE APPLE BLOSSOM COTTAGE STATS

DIMENSIONS: 27'8" long × 13'2" wide × 10'6" tall

SQUARE FOOTAGE: House: 264; porch: 48

BUDGET: $65,000

HEATING/COOLING: Propane direct-vent wall-mount Rinnai heater, with electric backup; wall-mount electric air conditioner

BATHROOM: Standard flush toilet to septic system; shower

POWER: Grid-tied (100 amp)

HOT WATER: Tankless propane water heater

Inspiration:
"Founder Jeff Wilson lived in a converted dumpster for a year to truly discover and examine small-space living and efficiency — and to later work his knowledge and experience into this design."

The Kasita

AUSTIN, TEXAS

DESIGN:
The Kasita team

THE KASITA HAS OUTSIZED FUNCTIONALITY in an under-sized footprint. From ceiling to floor, every last cubic inch is designed to maximize the dweller's experience. The result: "an exceptional small home that contains everything you need and nothing you don't." At least this is what Kasita's company website says. While those are big claims, there's no denying that this is one beautiful modern microdwelling, and with its technological enhancements, it's sure to tickle a geek's fancy.

"Smart technology" controls almost every element from heat to lighting, and the front window bay offers five levels of glass opacity, ranging from clear to "total blackout." This is something I've never, ever seen in a tiny house, so consider me impressed. When it comes to appliances, the Kasita comes stocked with them all: an induction cooktop, an induction oven, a washer and dryer, and even a dishwasher. Kasita is also branding these as the only tiny houses that are stackable, making it possible to have a sort of rack of apartments. Such a setup would allow occupants, when they decide to move, to simply have their unit craned out and inserted into another apartment facility elsewhere. While this hasn't been done just yet, and while, technically, shipping container houses are certainly stackable as well, there is a classy, futuristic elegance in this design that I rarely see with the units' shipping-box counterparts.

Wowed yet? If not, Kasita is also working on a system of interchangeable wall tiles, allowing the occupant to change the tiles' color and pattern as desired. While the style of this little house might not be for everyone, it is a very well-thought-out place. This may come as no surprise when you learn that, according to Kasita helmsman Jeff Wilson, more than 5,000 hours of engineering work went into it.

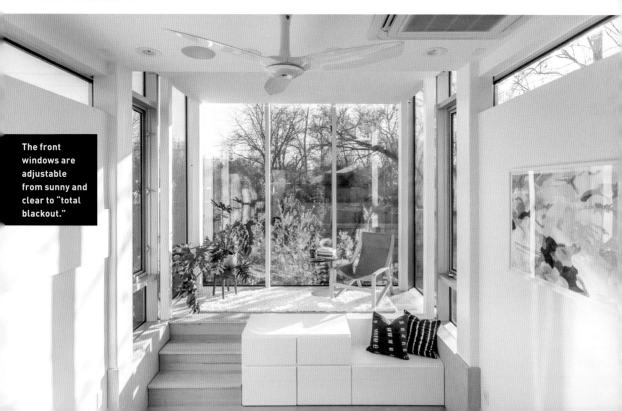

The front windows are adjustable from sunny and clear to "total blackout."

Yes, there is a bed — it pulls out from underneath the couch, trundle-style, much like the storage drawers that double as stairs in this three-tiered dwelling.

Of course, such gadgetry comes with a higher price tag, but designers like Kasita aren't aiming at the "I built my home for $3,000 out of old pallet wood" crowd. Think, rather, of the microflats of Paris or the modern mini apartments of Reykjavik, Iceland, and you'll get the vibe here: minimalism but with high-end materials and no skimping.

The front glass room, or "perch," is pretty striking, pretty gutsy (never mind expensive), and visually impressive. However, while the Kasita features climate control, I wonder how much solar gain you might expect in a place like Austin, Texas.

The high ceilings, the long and open feel, and the elevated kitchen space? Love 'em! The Kasita also features a flat-screen entertainment unit, for those who want to live like the Jetsons. It rises out of the storage unit near the front of the home at the push of a button (but of course!).

IN RETROSPECT:

"We continue to improve our design based on user feedback."

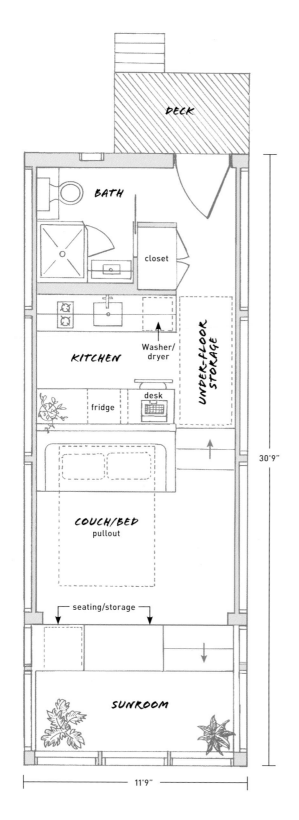

DECK

BATH

closet

KITCHEN

Washer/dryer

UNDER-FLOOR STORAGE

fridge

desk

COUCH/BED
pullout

seating/storage

SUNROOM

30'9"

11'9"

THE KASITA STATS

DIMENSIONS: 30'9" long × 11'9" wide × 12'6" high

SQUARE FOOTAGE: 330

BUDGET: $139,000

HEATING/COOLING: Electric mini split

BATHROOM: Standard flush toilet to septic or sewer; shower

POWER: Grid-tied

HOT WATER: Tankless hot water system

The Engberg Tiny House

SAN FRANCISCO,
CALIFORNIA

DESIGN:
Joshua and Shelley Engberg
of Tiny House Basics, LLC

DECIDING TO INCLUDE THE DESIGN WORK of Joshua and Shelley Engberg in this collection was a no-brainer. I was striving for a balance of funky, rustic, low-cost, and "out-there" builds, but at the same time I wanted to showcase some higher-end, more luxurious ones. Lo and behold, the Engbergs' design came along and satisfied both cravings.

From the tasteful placement of vibrant colors (that pop of teal sets such a fun vibe from the get-go) to the high-ceilinged open design, the Engberg home feels usable, welcoming, and attractive. Clean lines, a calming color palette, and the flowing layout help the space feel larger. The kitchen ranks among the best I've seen, a short list that includes another high-end tiny build from Michelle Boyle (page 133) as well as the work of Travis Pyke and his crew over at Wind River Tiny Homes (page 73). I often remind people not to "hate" the more expensive luxury homes but rather to look to them for ideas — lots and lots of ideas. Then you can use them to design your own home on a budget more suited to you.

Inspiration: "Everything under the sun. We drew a lot of inspiration from New Zealand tiny houses and the entertaining kitchens we saw that were filling the boards on Pinterest. Our design really centered around the accordion window and the idea of having an open and airy floor plan."

Windows, high ceilings, and vibrant highlights help this home stand out from the crowd.

The eight-foot accordion window is great for indoor/ outdoor entertaining.

The huge accordion service window that connects the kitchen to the outside deck is an online favorite, but it's the bright highlights — with just enough wildness — that really drew me to this build. A space like this is a photographer's dream, especially with its multitude of windows. Light and ventilation are unbelievably important in a tiny house. Windows and doors are also among the first things approaching guests will see and are integral to a home's overall beauty. Take your time in this department.

The kitchen's Pullman-style (aisle-like) arrangement makes it very user-friendly. Everything is in reach, but it doesn't feel claustrophobic. Open space, or at least the illusion of open space, is key in these incredibly small homes. I've seen many people cram so much stuff and so many dividing walls into their dwelling that it ends up feeling like a cramped cell. "The Alcatraz Tiny House" probably isn't what you're going for.

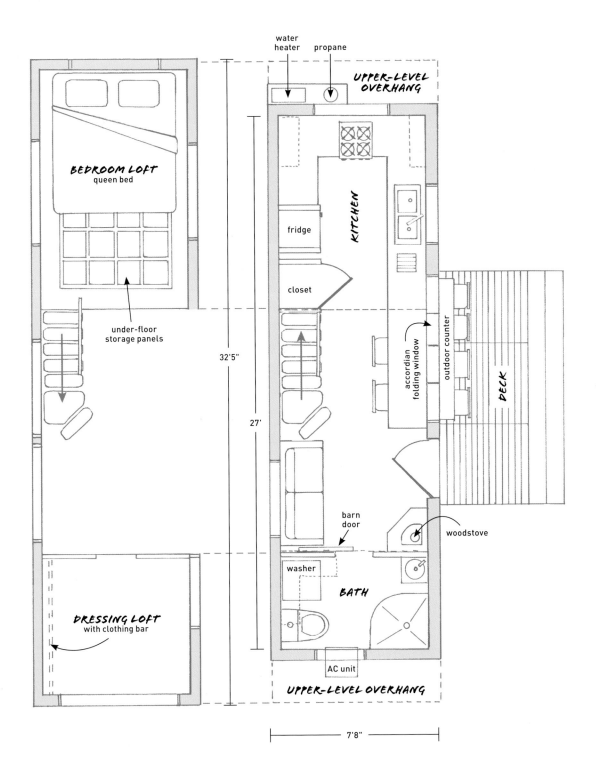

water heater
propane

UPPER-LEVEL OVERHANG

BEDROOM LOFT
queen bed

KITCHEN

fridge

closet

under-floor
storage panels

32'5"

27'

outdoor counter

accordian
folding window

DECK

barn
door

washer

woodstove

BATH

DRESSING LOFT
with clothing bar

AC unit

UPPER-LEVEL OVERHANG

7'8"

IN RETROSPECT: "If we could change anything we probably would have made the trailer a bit longer. At the time 28 feet for a tiny house was considered huge, but I'm sure a few extra feet would go a long way. Other than that, we wouldn't change a thing."

THE ENGBERG TINY HOUSE STATS

DIMENSIONS: 32' long × 8'11" wide × 13'6" tall; trailer is 28' long

SQUARE FOOTAGE: Ground level: 224; total, including lofts: 374

BUDGET: $80,000–$90,000

HEATING/COOLING: Kimberly woodstove; Envi wall heater; 12,000 Btu mini split

BATHROOM: Separett Villa composting toilet; shower

POWER: Grid-tied, with solar planned for the future

HOT WATER: Rinnai tankless electric water heater

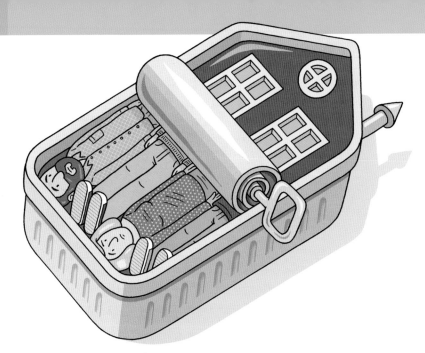

It Isn't for Everyone

ANDREW ODOM

I remember a number of afternoons growing up when I was under my dad's supervision. He was a contractor, so I would just tag along after him. Each day, we headed home for a little lunch. Some days it was a bologna sandwich. Other days it was a handful of Cheetos and a glass of tea. But at least once a week he would grab a ripe banana, slice it shortways with his pocket knife, and place each sliver on a piece of bread already slathered with mayonnaise. I would look at him crossly and continue to search the cupboards for something more appetizing. He would be at least halfway done with his "sammy" before saying I should just sit down and have a banana sandwich. My daddy loved those banana sandwiches. I loathed them. Some things aren't for everyone.

In 2010 my wife and I were in search of a home. Having both grown up in the South, we knew that because we were married, had jobs, and had a (meager) secure income, the next step in our American Dream was to obtain a starter house. We were scared to take such a financial leap of faith, though, and decided instead to research other options. That is when we stumbled across tiny homes on wheels. They were cute. They were mobile. And they complemented our bank account. Within days we were making our first napkin sketches of our future home.

We drew out a nice kitchen, a bedroom, and a multipurpose area that would serve as living room, dining room, and office. We felt like our tiny house, at 30 feet long, would be a tremendous asset for the next few years. But after the fourth month of our build, we found out we were pregnant, moving through the American Dream at breakneck speed. We stuck to our plan, though, and with a bit of creativity and brainstorming we had squeezed in a small nursery.

We moved into our tiny house on wheels in late 2011, just after having our daughter. We felt like aristocrats in our modest castle. Plus, we gained a new closeness. When my wife would be preparing a meal in the kitchen, she would stand against the counter at the stove, which was directly across from the refrigerator. If I wanted a drink out of the fridge, I couldn't get one without literally brushing up against her. That simple fact did more for our marriage than multiple sessions with any counselor or therapist.

We also developed an ability to find multiple uses for everything and an appreciation for the versatility of a single pair of jeans. We enjoyed the convenience of being able to reach almost everything without leaving the comfort of our bed. But after seven months, we began to long for something different.

As the weather turned cold and we found ourselves inside more than ever before, our 240-square-foot home became less quaint. It wasn't really that we wanted or needed more room. It was just that we grew weary of sitting still and staring out the same windows, hearing the same noises, and walking the same tired paths on the floor.

My wife and I had met as full-time missionaries on the mission field. Collectively we have lived in 9 countries and 11 states. For years both of us lived out of a backpack measured in cubic inches. We were no strangers to capsule wardrobes and minimal possessions, but we were strangers to sitting still. It was a rude awakening. We had quickly risen to the top of the tiny house world, and our popularity had spread across the Internet. We were a "tiny house family" and a successful one at that. We were living legally and raising a baby and still able to say we loved each other. But by nightfall each day we were restless. Our conversations turned to talk of travel.

I finally said to my bride, "You know, honey, tiny house living isn't for everyone." Even as I said it, I was imagining my dad, smiling and chewing, as he tried without success to get me to succumb to a banana sandwich.

Ultimately, tiny house living wasn't for us, at least not then, and probably not now. But we can't say that in the future when we are empty nesters it won't be ideal once again. Having your world literally at your fingertips is very cool. Being able to touch your

We decided to sell our tiny house on wheels and move on to our next adventure . . .

walls while just turning in circles is entertaining, if nothing else. But it might not be, probably isn't, most assuredly isn't, for everyone.

We decided to sell our tiny house on wheels and move on to our next adventure: a more traditional RV and a life on the road. We were told we were selling out and upsetting the order of things. People would email us and tell us our daughter would suffer for not having a home. In the beginning I allowed it to bother me, but after a few weeks I began to write back with the following:

"Tiny house living isn't for everyone. But being safe and comfortable in your home should be the right of anyone."

In those few words I found what I had started discovering in our tiny house and continued to find through our further adventures. I found freedom. We realized that our decision was part of our family's development. Some may call it a mistake. I look at it as a crucial part of growing up and growing into the life we were meant to live. Had we not built and lived in the tiny house, we might never have found out about composting toilets, under-floor storage, renewable energy, and so much more. That time in our tiny house was essential to who we are today.

After two years of living on the road, we realized that full-time RV life wasn't for us, either. Our daughter had become a little girl. I began working from home. My wife became more serious about her desire to cook and create in the kitchen. We sold our travel trailer and moved into a small house of just 900 square feet but with 2 acres of cleared land. We were able to return to our love of gardening and self-provision. Point is, tiny house living wasn't for us. But neither was RV life. And for all we know, our current situation might not be, either. That's okay, though, because I believe life isn't meant to be a one-chapter book.

Thinking back to what drew us to the tiny house life in the first place, I am reminded of the photo of Jay Shafer that I first saw on Tiny House Blog. Here was this guy, posing in front of an impossibly small home (being towed by a U-Haul truck, no less), arms crossed, a smile from ear to ear. It was as if he knew a secret. But when I think of that photo now, I am reminded that what really drew me to the tiny house life was not the house at all. It was what the house represented. That little Tumbleweed Fencl model and the man who owned it were a picture of freedom, of adventure, of disregard for conventionalism, and of an overwhelming sense of place.

No matter where we live, our lives should be all of those things. We deserve to be happy. We deserve to live in a home that reflects who we are. We deserve to throw caution to the wind and live in a home that is one part Seuss and one part Levitt, if we like. But above all, we deserve to live our own lives.

Before you build a tiny house or buy a tiny house on wheels or move to Alaska to build a trapper's cabin, ask yourself the following:

- **Does this house speak to me?**

- **Can I afford this house?**

- **Will I own this house or will it own me?**

- **Will I be able to leave this house as easily as I entered it?**

- **Do I care what others think?**

If you can honestly answer those questions without a pit of despair welling up inside you, then go for it.

Build your tiny house on wheels. Live the r(E)volution!

Not too long ago, my mom and dad were visiting our home, and he and I were outside working on my barn. Lunchtime rolled around. We went inside laughing and horsing around. Like an eagle's, my dad's eyes locked on to the three remaining bananas on the counter. "Son," he asked, "is your mayo in the fridge?" I told him it was and watched as he began making a banana sandwich. I went for the peanut butter and jelly. He noticed me just before he began to peel the banana and said, "Never mind. I'll have one of those." He started to put the banana away. I told him to grab that banana and make himself one heck of a sandwich.

> **We deserve to live in a home that reflects who we are.**

*Dweller, builder, author, host, and pontificator **Andrew M. Odom** — originally of **Tiny r(E)volution** — is a tiny houser with big ideas for the future of American housing.*

Jess and Dan's Homestead on Wheels

RHODE ISLAND

DESIGN:
Jess and Dan Sullivan

JESS AND DAN'S DEN, a fairly hidden tiny house deep in the acreage of an old farm, is a prime example of budget-building with salvaged materials. I simply love that this duo kept things so down-to-earth and simple. This box-like build utilizes as much vertical space as possible while avoiding crammed-in storage closets, multiple sleep levels, and odd nooks and cabinets in every available corner, all of which might otherwise kill the open look and feel of any home. There is an art to this fine balance, and Jess and Dan, in my estimation, have the knack.

It wouldn't be fair not to mention the ceiling of the home, which is sourced from the side of a barn built in 1776! Look closely and you'll see the holes and heads of old-fashioned square-cut nails.

The tiki-style loft ladder is a simple build made from local materials; it's fun, and it works. I will be honest and also state that such ladders can be a pain to climb and tough on bare feet. The same goes for dowel-rung ladders.

DEEK'S TAKEAWAYS

There is so much more going on inside this house than meets the eye. For one, the dividing wall between Jess's office nook and the closet is a vintage door with glass panes that once resided in her grandmother's home (no big-box-store wall paneling here). By using this door as a wall, the couple not only saved money and kept the door out of the landfill, they also created a conversation piece and a clever means to bring light into a small closet.

As for the outside, the fairly sizable deck by the home's entrance takes full advantage of a beautiful backwoods pond view and adds some outdoor living space. This is something I recommend in almost any climate. The tradeoff of price and time is well worth it. Furthermore, I recommend building the deck before the house, as it then gives you a handy flat place for doing your framing and all your future carpentry.

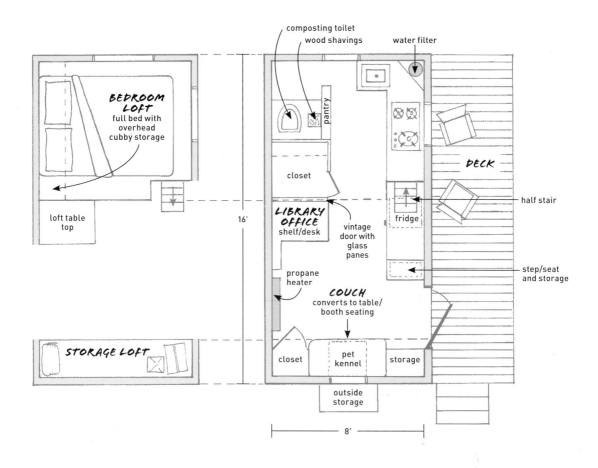

composting toilet
wood shavings

water filter

BEDROOM LOFT
full bed with overhead cubby storage

pantry

DECK

loft table top

16'

closet

half stair

LIBRARY OFFICE
shelf/desk

vintage door with glass panes

fridge

propane heater

COUCH
converts to table/ booth seating

step/seat and storage

STORAGE LOFT

closet

pet kennel

storage

outside storage

8'

IN RETROSPECT:

"I'd take the time to learn a few more skills and tricks in basic cabinetry. I always felt that the storage in the kitchen could have been way more efficient. Also, make sure all windows in the loft can open wide. Ventilation is key on hot days, and one of our windows was able to open only a couple of inches."

JESS AND DAN'S HOMESTEAD ON WHEELS STATS

DIMENSIONS: 16' long × 8'6" wide × 10' tall

SQUARE FOOTAGE: Main area: 160; loft: 50

BUDGET: $13,000

HEATING/COOLING: Direct-vent propane heater

BATHROOM: Homemade composting toilet; outdoor solar shower stall

POWER: Fully solar and off-grid

HOT WATER: Carried in, stored in water "bricks," and heated on the stove as needed for food prep and washing

Inspiration:
"Tumbleweed Tiny House Company plans and a desire to be debt-free."
—*Brittany*

Brittany's Bayside Bungalow

OLYMPIA, WASHINGTON

DESIGN:
Tumbleweed
Tiny House Company
(with Brittany Yunker's spin
on a few things)

WALK THROUGH THE DOORS of this Tumbleweed Tiny House Company Cypress model, and you'll quickly find yourself in a place of serenity and relaxation. This space works, thanks to the colors, the uninterrupted layout, and the cathedral ceiling that cheats the mind into thinking it is far more grand than it really is. While the high ceiling might seem like a waste of space (instead of building a second loft level or overhead storage), it is actually a useful demonstration of restraint in the tiny house world.

As many tiny houses do, Brittany's Bayside Bungalow employs a galley-style kitchen. Not only does this area double as a hallway to the bathroom, it also keeps everything within reach without gobbling up too much of the house's overall footprint. The light colors of the kitchen and the home overall add to the feeling of greater space and height. A view of Puget Sound and its shoreline forests doesn't hurt, either.

DEEK'S TAKEAWAYS

As a fan of artistic chaos, I hate to admit it, but the "less is more" approach works here. This bungalow doesn't come close to overdoing it with art and decor, yet everywhere you look, there is something eye-pleasing, interesting, and fun. Brittany has even made her necessary and everyday items, such as her kitchen sink, stand as artistic pieces themselves.

I must also give the "Triple B" and Tumbleweed a further nod when it comes to the seating nook. Some say that the mini exterior porch (the plans come both with or without) is a waste of square footage, but it not only creates a dry overhang where you can fumble for your keys or hang a plant but also produces a more visually appealing entrance than the "flat door in a giant flat wall" look. As a by-product, the mini seating nook, with its oversized windows, is the coziest space in Brittany's home. In fact, I worked there on my laptop while enjoying several gallons of coffee.

The kitchen sink is a work of art.

Coffee sacks make a fun replacement for cabinet doors and don't require swing space.

IN RETROSPECT: "Light colors can be tough to keep clean, especially with heavy traffic and visitors, but the look does keep things feeling light and open. Also, the open-shelf approach in the kitchen is pleasing to the eye and forces you to keep things orderly, but it can also limit your storage — it's a double-edged sword."

BRITTANY'S BAYSIDE BUNGALOW STATS

DIMENSIONS: 19'5" long × 8'6" wide × 13'6" tall

SQUARE FOOTAGE: Main area: approximately 160; loft: 60

BUDGET: $18,000 (Brittany bought the plans and built it herself)

HEATING/COOLING: Envi electric wall heater; infrared outlet heater (plugs into an electrical outlet); Dickinson Marine Newport P1200 Propane Fireplace

BATHROOM: Composting toilet (homemade, with urine diverter); shower

POWER: Grid-tied (to main house nearby)

HOT WATER: Tankless propane water heater (mounted to kitchen wall)

The Dickinson propane fireplace, originally made for the nautical world, has caught on with many tiny house dwellers.

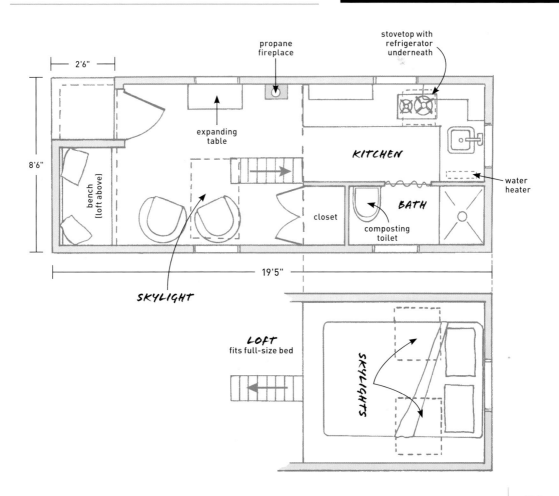

propane fireplace

stovetop with refrigerator underneath

2'6"

8'6"

bench (loft above)

expanding table

KITCHEN

water heater

closet

BATH

composting toilet

19'5"

SKYLIGHT

LOFT
fits full-size bed

SKYLIGHTS

Inspiration:
"What the client wanted, with class and color."

Topographical hiking maps make creative wallpaper.

The Wind River Airstream

CHATTANOOGA,
TENNESSEE

DESIGN:
Travis Pyke
and the Wind River
Tiny Homes crew

THIS JAW-DROPPING AIRSTREAM was magnificently brought back to life by Travis Pyke and his crew at Wind River Tiny Homes. The 24-foot 1974 Airstream Overlander was delivered to them with its entire floor rotted out and its steel undercarriage in desperate need of re-welding and strengthening. Well, about five billion hours later (not quite, but they ended up exceeding their time budget and working almost three weeks for free) they arrived at the reborn trailer you see here. This flip, almost a work of art, is fun and daring, yet not quite over-the-top. It's the simplest approaches, such as the use of free pallet wood, that make this dwelling pop.

Pallet wood is now so popular that it's sold in fake-old form at chain stores, but it's still very easy to procure for free. In fact, many industrial operations put it out on the roadside and encourage people to take it. The Wind River folks even went so far as to apply the wood to the curves of this Airstream's ceiling by meticulously making shallow cuts into the backside of the wood to make it thinner and more pliable. It's a simple method but takes a boatload of motivation and patience. Add in a comfy and attractive custom daybed, mid-century modern touches, and a light-filled, attractive, and usable bathroom, and you have the recipe for something truly awe-inspiring.

The bathroom door is a gorgeous and effective focal point, as is the real-deal porthole window.

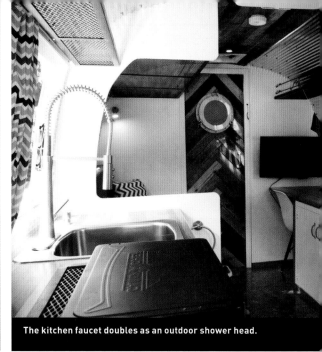

The kitchen faucet doubles as an outdoor shower head.

DEEK'S TAKEAWAYS

I'd be hard-pressed to find anything I don't like here. One good educational takeaway for those planning their own small homes is the great implementation of "dual usage" in the Wind River crew's work. You'll hear about this technique over and over in the world of tiny housing. Examples include the slatted daybed near the bathroom that pulls out into sleeping space for two, and the sprayer hose in the kitchen sink that can swivel around, extend out through the adjacent window, and become an outdoor shower. The sink-sprayer-turned-outdoor-shower is standard on some camper models and is a great feature to emulate.

"Funk on a budget" is also on full display here, with topographical hiking maps being used as wallpaper on one end of the Airstream. It saves money, reuses old materials, is a neat conversation piece, and just looks great!

The couch/day bed pulls out into sleep space for two.

Be your funky self.

IN RETROSPECT:

"It took so long. We didn't realize how many hours and how much work would have to go into a project like this, but we were pleased with the results. It became a labor of love, and I think that shows. The complex compound cuts needed to reframe and replace windows and wall work were a huge chore, too — some had to be done by trial and error. Any DIY future builder should realize that their project will take much longer than they anticipate. Plan for delays and mistakes and always ready yourself for the unexpected, and you won't be as stressed and frustrated. The sooner you learn this, the better off you'll be."

Corrugated aluminum panels help give this flip a modern feel.

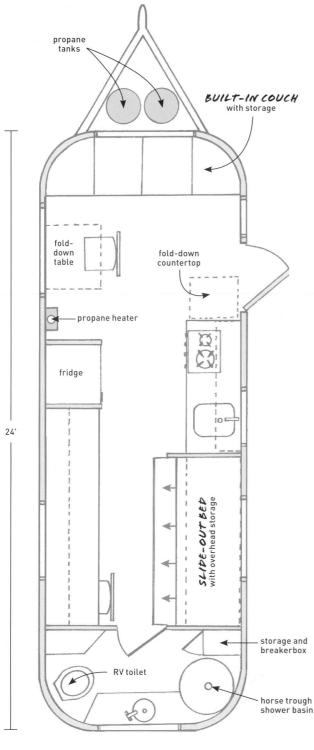

propane tanks

BUILT-IN COUCH
with storage

fold-down table

fold-down countertop

propane heater

fridge

24'

SLIDE-OUT BED
with overhead storage

storage and breakerbox

RV toilet

horse trough shower basin

8'6"

THE WIND RIVER AIRSTREAM STATS

DIMENSIONS: 24' long × 8'6" wide × 7'6" tall

SQUARE FOOTAGE: 190

BUDGET: $50,000 (the Airstream was $2,500; no profit was made)

HEATING/COOLING: Dometic Penguin II Heat Pump (for heating and cooling); Dickinson Marine Newport P1200 Propane Fireplace

BATHROOM: Dometic 310 RV toilet; shower

POWER: RV cord hookup

HOT WATER: Atwood 6-gallon propane water heater

The Alpha Tiny House

NASHVILLE/
CHATTANOOGA,
TENNESSEE

DESIGN:
David Latimer and
Zac Thomas,
New Frontier Tiny Homes

Inspiration:
"Zen temples and
sculpture gardens,
Japanese tea houses,
Scandinavian cabins
and micro apartments,
utilitarian beauty,
uncompromising dual
priorities of beauty and
utility in everything,
New York and Parisian
microflats."

WELCOME BACK TO THE LUXURY REALM of tiny houses. This particular work, from Nashville-based team David Latimer and Zac Thomas, took only seven weeks to build — impressive for such high quality. While a good deal of money was invested in this undertaking, it wasn't spent frivolously. To kick things off, you're greeted with a fold-down deck. This is not anything new, but it's the first drop-deck I've seen that also serves as in-transit protection for what has to be one of the larger tiny house "windows" out there: an industrial glass garage door. Remember that Ferrari house in *Ferris Bueller's Day Off*? Well, that's this home, more or less, but on wheels (and a heck of a lot smaller). Generally, I'm not much for luxury builds, but there is no getting around how sleek, modern, and friggin' gorgeous this place is.

Step inside through the enormous 9 × 8-foot sliding doors, and you'll set your eyes on granite countertops, a calico array of vintage barn wood on the ceiling, and, best of all, secret drop-down storage bins recessed between the ceiling joists. When locked in place, their plank-clad sides mesh perfectly with the ceiling, so you'd never even know to look for them.

The bathroom is definitely drool-worthy. It harbors a washer and dryer unit and a full-size tub with Jacuzzi jets! All in all, there really is no sacrifice here, and yet the structure is less than one-eighth the size of the average American house. Did I mention the five-burner induction cooktop with a vented hood? David and Zac, you've outdone yourselves.

The garage door slides up and down to create a versatile indoor/outdoor space.

DEEK'S TAKEAWAYS

Aside from the cost of a high-end build like this (don't think this is what you'll end up with on a $3,000 budget and a pile of pallets your friend gave you), keep in mind solar gain and heat loss if you are considering huge windows. Sun exposure will quickly heat up a space like this during the day, and the large expanses of glass will likely make it cold at night, depending on the climate and the orientation of the home. Even well-sealed thermal windows have very low R-value compared to an insulated wall. So there's another tip: know your land and your building site before you break ground or park your home. And if you're planning to take your house on the road, be sure to use tempered glass for both your safety and that of others. (Tempered glass is more impact-resistant than standard glass, and it shatters into small pieces rather than large shards.)

I'll also add that I love the "step-up" kitchen and roll-out storage benches as well as the folding table that comes out of this sub-kitchen space — it's rather genius. My only warning about a similar setup would be to make sure your seating and table don't use up all of your standing space or block access to the kitchen or other living areas.

The kitchen's 33-inch farmhouse apron sink crushes all stereotypes that tiny houses must have tiny sinks.

Storage benches and a folding table roll out from underneath the kitchen.

IN RETROSPECT:

"In all honesty, I wouldn't say I have any regrets or mistakes. What some may see as mistakes, I see more as learning opportunities. I'm also as OCD as the Rain Man. So I'd simply offer that planning, and then planning some more, is a very good idea.

"There are a few variations I've made to other iterations of the Alpha: I've added a futon or bed under the dining table, and I've split one of the benches into two separate benches and built little stool boxes inside. Additionally, I tweaked the nesting set table design to be more user-friendly and increased the length of the trailer size by 2 feet, which allowed for a larger closet and more space in the loft without causing you to duck the garage door track."

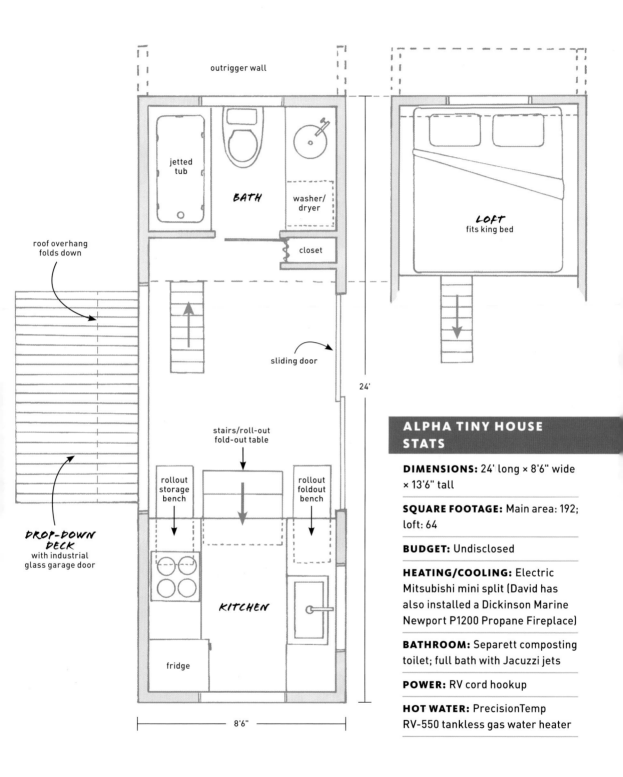

outrigger wall

jetted tub

BATH

washer/ dryer

closet

LOFT
fits king bed

roof overhang
folds down

sliding door

24'

stairs/roll-out
fold-out table

rollout
storage
bench

rollout
foldout
bench

DROP-DOWN
DECK
with industrial
glass garage door

KITCHEN

fridge

8'6"

ALPHA TINY HOUSE STATS

DIMENSIONS: 24' long × 8'6" wide × 13'6" tall

SQUARE FOOTAGE: Main area: 192; loft: 64

BUDGET: Undisclosed

HEATING/COOLING: Electric Mitsubishi mini split (David has also installed a Dickinson Marine Newport P1200 Propane Fireplace)

BATHROOM: Separett composting toilet; full bath with Jacuzzi jets

POWER: RV cord hookup

HOT WATER: PrecisionTemp RV-550 tankless gas water heater

Inspiration:
"We were hugely inspired by 'Outside Found.' I love their bus, and their adventures seemed so magical."

The Puckett House Bus

STONE MOUNTAIN, GEORGIA

DESIGN:
Julie Puckett,
Andrew Puckett,
Tom Gibbs,
and Beth Gibbs

B US CONVERSIONS, OR "SKOOLIES" (and yes, it is spelled that way), have been around for ages. They became popular in the 1960s and '70s, and recently more and more of them seem to be popping up. Here we have a shining example of how a bus conversion can be a more affordable alternative to the traditional tiny house while also being absolutely jaw-dropping. The Pucketts' 30-foot Bluebird school bus was initially a solution to the high rent the duo was paying in Atlanta. Little more than a shell at first, it soon bloomed into an actual home. With its open layout, light colors, living room space, and the book-lined bedroom (they fit *lots* of books in here) loaded with storage, this is no stereotypical "grungy hippie bus."

The Pucketts' bus, in its careful minimalism, is part rolling house, part art. Even things like the bright pops of light from two IKEA hanging lamps add a tiny yet daring drop of color and fun to the space. The Pucketts definitely aren't roughing it, either. They have a kitchen space with ample storage, an oven and range, a large flat-screen TV, a woodstove, a table that transforms into a crate space for their dog, and a long couch complete with storage underneath that will comfortably sleep almost any adult.

Woodstove

IN RETROSPECT: "We chose an inexpensive bus that needed a lot of expensive repairs to make it a feasible travel option. We were up against the clock, and our choice of bus reflected that. But it made traveling difficult, which was partly the point of living in a bus in the first place. Make sure you really know your stuff and look over that bus (or trailer, if you're building a tiny house) before you make that purchase, never mind pick up a hammer."

DEEK'S TAKEAWAYS

The advantage to starting with a bus, or a shipping container (see pages 119 and 153), is that you immediately have an enclosed, watertight (you hope) shell for your home. You also have a safe, lockable space to store your tools overnight. On the other hand, insulating and building against a curved roof is difficult, and your ceiling height is limited. No tiny house approach or solution is perfect, but these conversions are a noteworthy option for the budget-minded.

On the detail level, I'm a fan of the cabinet drawers on tracks, which allow easy access to the backs of cabinets without disrupting the contents in the front. The shower walls lined with metal roofing are a nice touch, for both aesthetics and budget. And there's an abundance of clever space hacks in here, such as the butcher block top that fits over the stove to extend the counter space when the range isn't in use. It's tricks like these that make small spaces more livable.

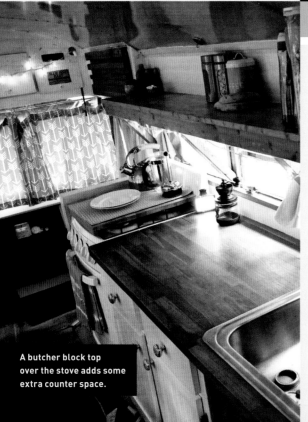

A butcher block top over the stove adds some extra counter space.

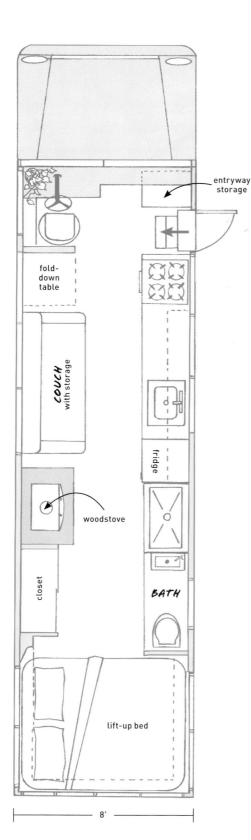

entryway
storage

fold-
down
table

COUCH
with storage

30'

woodstove

closet

fridge

BATH

lift-up bed

8'

THE PUCKETT HOUSE
BUS STATS

DIMENSIONS: 30' long × 8' wide × 10'5" tall

SQUARE FOOTAGE: Just under 200 livable square feet

BUDGET: $10,000

HEATING/COOLING: Woodstove for extreme cold, in addition to a space heater that's usually enough for Georgia's mild winters

BATHROOM: Shower and the Thetford Curve, a two-compartment, closed-system toilet with a water reservoir on top and a waste reservoir in the bottom. It has a battery-operated flush, and when the waste reservoir is full it disconnects from the top so it can be emptied.

POWER: RV cord hookup

HOT WATER: Tankless propane water heater

The detachable deck and Tuftex overhang make for a welcoming entrance.

The Alberta Modern Tiny House

PORTLAND, OREGON

DESIGN:
Ian Dorresteyn
and James Sterrett

Inspiration:
"Dee Williams and
the Portland
Alternative
Dwellings (PAD)
building group."

T **HIS TINY HOUSE ON WHEELS** was designed and built by schoolteachers Ian and Jessie Dorresteyn over two summers and many weekend-warrior pushes. All told, it came in at $17,000, a very meager budget considering the size of the house, the large windows, and the materials. What was their secret?

Reused and recycled materials played a huge part in this 24-foot build (26 if you count the triangular bathroom bump-out). In fact, the builders estimate that 80 percent of it was made from reclaimed materials, many of which came from a Restore. While reuse often goes hand in hand with additional labor — not to mention lots of planing, sanding, reconfiguring, and designing on the fly — for some, this is an enjoyable challenge and a way to infuse a home with character. And this house certainly lacks none of that.

Ian and Jessie wanted a sparse and modern feel, so they stowed their kitchen goods and attractive canning jars in the exposed framing (also reclaimed, with marks of antique square nail heads). The simple woodwork looks great, too, from the sliding bathroom door to the cabinets above the entryway.

The loft ladder hangs to the left of the front door.

DEEK'S TAKEAWAYS

On the outside of the home, Ian and Jessie broke up the flat wall of their entrance by recessing the entry 2½ feet and adding a detachable deck and small overhang made with Tuftex polycarbonate panels. This visual tactic creates a more gradual transition from outdoors to in, and the deck is perfect for Portland summers.

Talking with Ian, I soon realized that he and I share two design loves: single-pitched roofs and batten-strip interior siding. The single-pitch roof, as he sees, is easier to frame because it requires fewer cuts and angle work, and it's plenty strong and leaves lots of lofty interior space. The ceilings in Ian and Jessie's home are over 10 feet high, which goes a long way toward making the small space feel less claustrophobic. And as for the batten strips, they're just an old time-saving technique that, when done at even intervals, look good, too. In the case of the Alberta Modern, the interior siding is lightweight sheets of ¼-inch plywood, and where each sheet ends and another begins, a simple strip of wood covers the seam. No drywall mudding, no multitude of tongue-and-groove planks, just big ol' thin slabs of plywood. It's simple and it works.

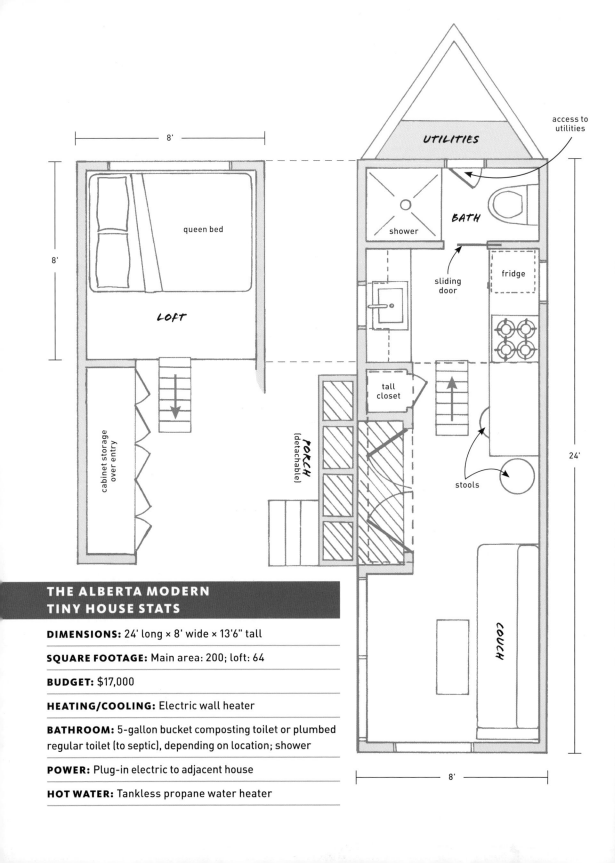

8'

8'

8'

queen bed

LOFT

cabinet storage over entry

UTILITIES

access to utilities

shower

BATH

sliding door

fridge

PORCH (detachable)

tall closet

stools

24'

COUCH

8'

THE ALBERTA MODERN TINY HOUSE STATS

DIMENSIONS: 24' long × 8' wide × 13'6" tall

SQUARE FOOTAGE: Main area: 200; loft: 64

BUDGET: $17,000

HEATING/COOLING: Electric wall heater

BATHROOM: 5-gallon bucket composting toilet or plumbed regular toilet (to septic), depending on location; shower

POWER: Plug-in electric to adjacent house

HOT WATER: Tankless propane water heater

IN RETROSPECT:
"I would not buy a three-season on-demand water heater. I mounted it in a well-vented compartment on the hitch, but it is very susceptible to freezing there and has caused problems. All else I've been more than pleased with."

The cabinet doors were chopped from a large, defunct garage door, though you'd never suspect it.

Bear's Tiny House

FARMINGTON, GEORGIA

DESIGN:
Mark Warfield

Inspiration:
"Tracy Lewis, a longtime family friend and tiny house enthusiast, kept prodding me to check out the scene. Well, I went to the 2016 Eatonton, Georgia, Tiny House Festival, got hooked, and built my first house starting in June of 2016."

MARK "BEAR" WARFIELD is a man who doesn't mess around. I could see this the minute I set foot inside his tiny home while it was on display in Florida. He doesn't bother with bells and whistles, and this is why I was attracted to his design. While the shape of the home, with its traditional gable look, might not particularly stand out, the interior speaks volumes. In the TV era of high-priced, ultra-modern homes decked out with stainless steel and gadgetry galore, Bear chose to stick to his North Carolina backwoods roots and keep things warm, natural, and "countrified."

For starters, the entire interior of the house is covered in eastern white pine (no paints, dark stains, or color-altering synthetic applications — just a glossy clear coat). This immediately gives you a feel for what Bear's Tiny Homes (Mark's company) is going for. But don't let the Adirondack quaintness fool you. This dual-axle, 24-foot-long beauty has a few other things that many tiny homes don't: a dishwasher, a slate-covered propane fireplace, a washer and dryer combo, a micro-wave, a four-burner gas range, and a full staircase to the loft. The master bedroom is downstairs, just beyond the bathroom. The handy thing about this design is that guests sleeping in the loft do not have to cut through the bedroom to get to the toilet. I can't tell you how many times I see the reverse.

This is another case where the open loft proves to be a better choice than one stuffed with storage and built-ins. Bear's home has a light and airy feel and space for a real-deal 8-foot couch (you rarely see that). It also features a great vintage triangular window in the loft that was salvaged from an old church, and one of the more attractive countertops I've ever seen in a tiny house.

Bear's custom-built shower is another case of clever simplicity, as it's merely a plywood stall with a rubberized coating called Granite Flex. It's tough, affordable, available in several shades, and, best of all, completely waterproof.

The one note of caution I have about this design is that stairs built too close to a gable roof can be hard to navigate as you get closer to that roof. I see this in many tiny homes, and while it's a problem that is frequently hard to avoid, it's something to keep in mind.

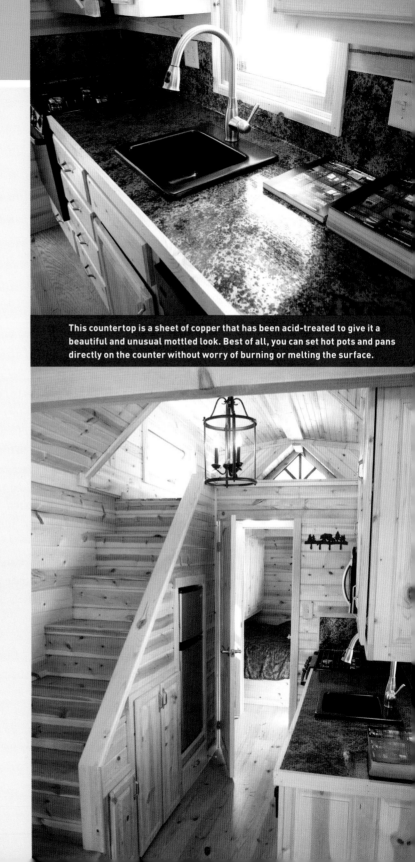

This countertop is a sheet of copper that has been acid-treated to give it a beautiful and unusual mottled look. Best of all, you can set hot pots and pans directly on the counter without worry of burning or melting the surface.

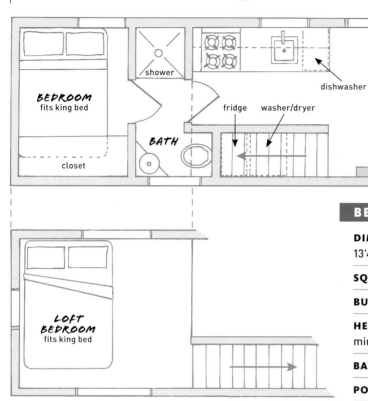

24'8"

8'6"

BEDROOM
fits king bed

closet

shower

BATH

fridge

washer/dryer

dishwasher

gas fireplace

DECK

LOFT
BEDROOM
fits king bed

BEAR'S TINY HOUSE STATS

DIMENSIONS: 24'8" long × 8'6" wide × 13'4" tall

SQUARE FOOTAGE: Main area: 200; loft: 56

BUDGET: $68,000

HEATING/COOLING: Dual-zone electric mini split; gas fireplace

BATHROOM: RV flush toilet; shower

POWER: 50-amp RV cord hookup

HOT WATER: Instant/on-demand electric

Inspiration: "Open space and a connection with the outdoors, while incorporating innovation."

Fold-down deck

Dragonfly Tiny House

REGINA, SASKATCHEWAN,
CANADA

DESIGN:
Robinson Residential Design

I USED TO NOT BE A FAN OF STARK MODERN DWELLINGS. Perhaps I've scanned too many issues of *Dwell* in airport lobbies or watched too many TV shows pushing this look, but now I'm somewhat head over heels for it (with a dash of punk-rock art chaos, mind you!). The key is to keep it clean and light without making it feel sterile and uncomfortable. Well, lucky for you and me, the Robinson brothers have nailed this look not only with the large residential homes they design but also with their first tiny house offering, the Dragonfly — named for its opposing decks that fold down like wings.

And how cool is this place?! Though only 20 feet long (and 160 square feet overall), it has a heck of an array of not-so-crammed-in features. These include a galley-style kitchen (counters on both sides), built-in shelving by a love seat near the entryway, tasteful open kitchen storage, and an ultra-ingenious kitchen table that pulls out from under the counters to provide additional dining and prep space. Finally, there's the artful touch of three stained glass windows — depicting dragonflies, of course.

The slide-out table, while incredibly clever, blocks off one entire patio door — but, of course, the Dragonfly has another patio door to spare. Much like David Latimer's Alpha house (page 79), the outdoor world is so present in this home that it almost seems to meld into the interior space. The fold-down decks are great, too.

I'm also a fan of the two-toned siding, which is less monotonous than using a single type of standard siding. By using more expensive siding (cedar, for example) in only key places, you can give your house a fancier look without spending the money to upgrade all of the siding. In the case of the Robinsons' house, they've pulled it off beautifully, while also adding some decorative wall and roof work.

Pull-out stairs to loft

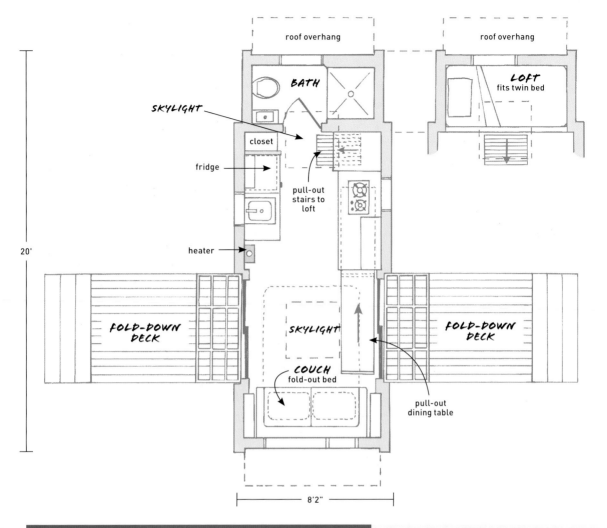

roof overhang

roof overhang

BATH

LOFT
fits twin bed

SKYLIGHT

closet

fridge

pull-out
stairs to
loft

heater

20'

FOLD-DOWN
DECK

SKYLIGHT

FOLD-DOWN
DECK

COUCH
fold-out bed

pull-out
dining table

8'2"

DRAGONFLY TINY HOUSE STATS

DIMENSIONS: 20' long × 8'2" wide × 13'6" tall

SQUARE FOOTAGE: Main area: 160; loft: 30

BUDGET: $52,500

HEATING/COOLING: Dickinson Marine Newport P1200 Propane Fireplace; there is natural cooling thanks to windows and high insulation value (by way of structural insulated panels, or SIPs)

BATHROOM: Nature's Head composting toilet; shower

POWER: Grid-tied 110-volt outlet setup; some lights are 12-volt, as are the heater and toilet fan

HOT WATER: Tank-style electric water heater (under the kitchen cabinets)

IN RETROSPECT:

"I think we would include a washer/dryer, since that seems to be a sticking point for some people — they don't want to do without one, even though it takes up a lot of space and requires additional power. This unit is very airtight, so in some climates an air-to-air heat exchanger would be good for bringing in fresh air and exhausting moisture."

Inspiration:
"The many desert
bottle houses
of yesteryears
and a love of
'making something
from nothing.'"

The Bottlerock House

JOSHUA TREE,
CALIFORNIA

DESIGN: Cary Ezell

BOTTLE HOUSES HAVE BEEN ON THE SCENE FOR AGES —
from the famous desert dwelling of Grandma Prisbrey to
Tom Kelly's house in Rhyolite, Nevada — and have a wide
appeal due to their looks and low cost. But these attractive structures
do come with a price: massive amounts of labor.

Cary Ezell, who began building this bottle house in 2007, claims that
his structure, an Airbnb rental perched right outside of Joshua Tree
National Park, is composed of no fewer than 7,500 bottles. Think
about that for a second. Cary hurdled the task of bottle collection with
a clever approach. "I put the word out to restaurants, friends, and
local businesses to save whatever bottles they could for me," he said.
"But I also told the homeless in my area that I'd pay them more than
market value for the glass if they'd bring it to me." By this method
he was not only helping down-on-their-luck citizens in his hometown
but also saving himself a load of work.

That was just the beginning, though. Each bottle in Cary's Bottlerock
House had to be cut with a tile saw into a 4-inch "end." Two ends were then
glued together with autoglass adhesive to form a single brick and laid
into the wall with mortar. But before any of that, Cary had to soak, clean,
and remove the labels from each and every wine and liquor bottle (beer
bottles are too thin). Did I mention there were 7,500 of them? And then
there was the framing, stonework, rebar layers, hardware ties, and the
mixing and mortar work. Bottlerock, without a doubt, was a labor of love.

DEEK'S TAKEAWAYS

The interior of this abode is sparse but funky. Cary seems to operate in a state of organized chaos, something I can identify with (and my wife can't). Just check out the Timothy-Leary-meets-Sanford-and-Son collection of old cars, vintage trailers, and Route 66 neon signs. The bottle walls certainly set the scene for the unconventional, but the 1950s-era travel trailer door (taken from a desert camper) solidifies the vibe. I've seen car doors, barn siding panels, and a slew of other makeshift door ideas, but the notion of borrowing an old camper door is so unprofound that it somehow comes off as semi-genius. Then again, finding such rare, odd, and attractive items takes a high level of skill and patience, not to mention the right eye — and Cary proves that he's no rookie.

The stone patio and porch are beautiful, but the translucent bottles are what literally shine. At night the bottle house radiates light, and in the daytime it takes it in. It's awe-inspiring.

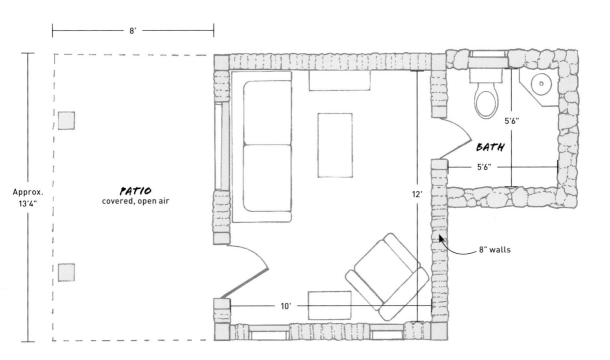

Approx. 13'4"

8'

PATIO
covered, open air

12'

10'

BATH

5'6"

5'6"

8" walls

THE BOTTLEROCK HOUSE STATS

DIMENSIONS: 10' × 12' base, approximately 12' tall

SQUARE FOOTAGE: Main room: 120; bathroom: 36

BUDGET: $3,500

HEATING/COOLING: None, other than the natural properties of the stone and mortar (thermal mass)

BATHROOM: Standard flush toilet to septic system; shower in the main house 30 feet away

POWER: Grid-tied

HOT WATER: None

IN RETROSPECT: "I wish I had made it more random and thrown in a few cool-looking rocks here and there instead of trying to make rows. But, honestly, I'm happy with the outcome. The only warning I would have is to be prepared to spend a ton of time cutting and gluing the ends [of bottles] together."

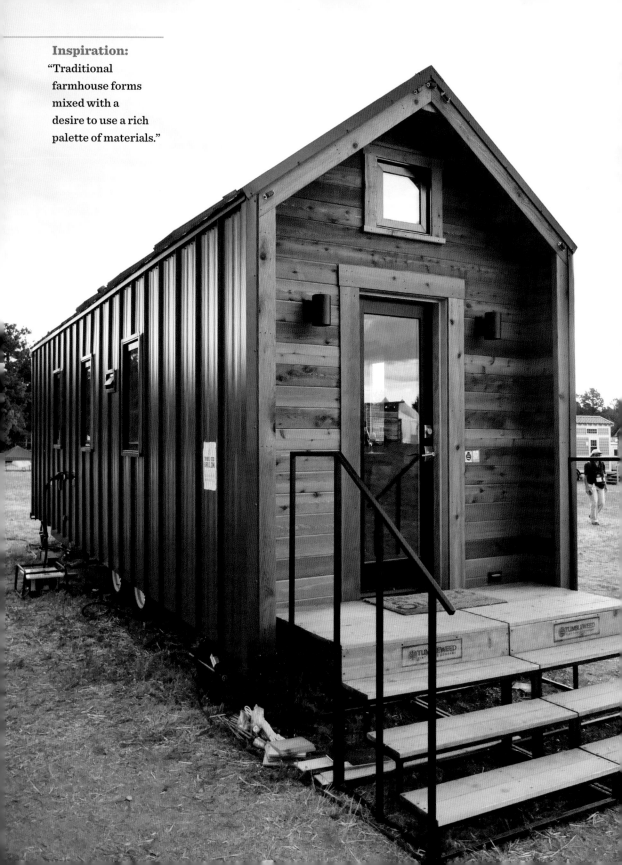

The Farallon

THE FARALLON, designed by Laura Schmitz under the Tumbleweed banner, turned plenty of heads when it came onto the scene in 2016. With a more modern look (much like Tumbleweed's Mica design), the Farallon is not only a larger tiny house but, following the current trend, a more luxurious one. Featuring a standing seam roof and walls to match, a washer-dryer combo, a three-quarter-height refrigerator, a farmer's apron sink, three skylights, a four-burner range, an electric fireplace, and even walnut countertops and stair treads, this one has it all.

While the early values of the tiny house phenomenon were about minimalism and sacrifice, this tiny house, and many others like it, are a step in a different direction. Most folks out there who are enamored with the idea of going small just aren't willing or ready to step into the more sparse and restrained version of tiny living. And there's nothing wrong with that. Make no mistake, this is a beautiful house, potentially the best that Tumbleweed has released. Just take a peek at the clever built-ins, the transforming IKEA Norbo table, the hidden heater and water tank under the stairs, the modern open-shelf storage, and its slick birch plywood walls. Coming in at 14,000 pounds and 26 feet in length, it may be large for a tiny house, but it still holds on tight to the "cute and classy" factor that so many tiny house fans are looking for. Cleverly, it also has three different versions of the floor plan to choose from.

Built-in shelving
and storage

Nature's Head
composting toilet

DEEK'S TAKEAWAYS

I'm sure you're thinking the same thing: finally, another
house option with a downstairs bedroom! And this
one is cozy and airy as well. Many people interested in
tiny houses are empty-nesters or are looking toward
retirement and want to cut back their expenses.
However, the prospect of climbing perilous ladders or
stairs in order to squeeze into a tiny loft may be a
deal-breaker. Here you get the best of both worlds:
a little downstairs bedroom adjacent to a bathroom in
the rear, in addition to a sleep loft. My only concern
with the lower bedroom layout is that guests would have
to cut through the bedroom to get to the bathroom.
Otherwise, I love this design on about 40 levels.

Apron
sink

Three-quarter-
height refrigerator

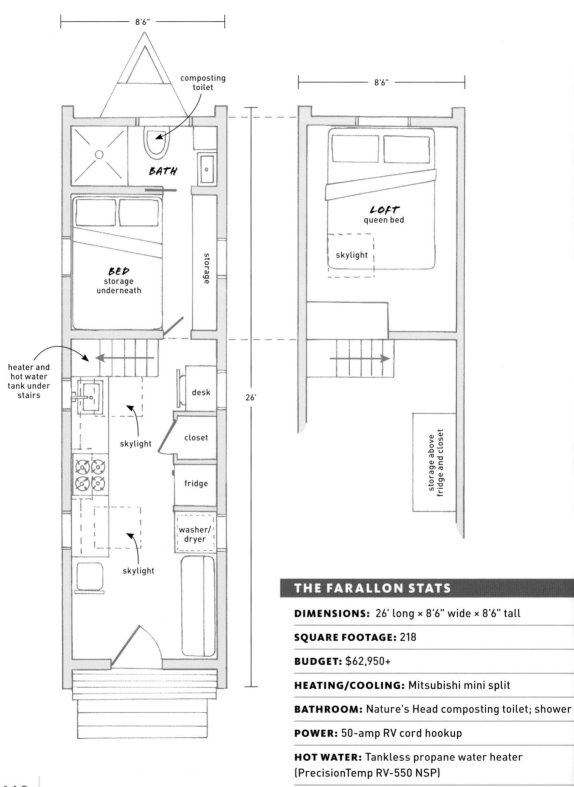

8'6"

composting
toilet

BATH

storage

BED
storage
underneath

heater and
hot water
tank under
stairs

skylight

desk

closet

fridge

washer/
dryer

skylight

8'6"

LOFT
queen bed

skylight

storage above
fridge and closet

26'

THE FARALLON STATS

DIMENSIONS: 26' long × 8'6" wide × 8'6" tall

SQUARE FOOTAGE: 218

BUDGET: $62,950+

HEATING/COOLING: Mitsubishi mini split

BATHROOM: Nature's Head composting toilet; shower

POWER: 50-amp RV cord hookup

HOT WATER: Tankless propane water heater
(PrecisionTemp RV-550 NSP)

IN RETROSPECT: "Initially (as shown below) we had no railing next to the stairs. We later added one to make sure that climbing into the upstairs loft was a bit easier and safer."

Walnut stair treads

The Shangri-Little

CHATTANOOGA,
TENNESSEE

DESIGN:
Brian Morris,
Mike Morris,
and Ozwaldo Lopez

THIS 8 × 24-FOOT WHEELED HOME was a collaboration between designer Brian Morris and a TV crew of contractors led by Zack Giffin of *Tiny House Nation*. Brian, like Vera Struck (page 199), was another one of our early workshop attendees. The Shangri-Little is part of a rental compound (Live a Little Chatt, co-run and owned by Morris and Joe Curro) that features four tiny homes, including the Alpha Tiny House (page 79), but this one might be my favorite in terms of layout.

For those looking for whimsy, function, and inventiveness, the Shangri-Little is a cornucopia of all that. While the roof deck with flip-up welded steel railings is a fan favorite, the single-slab hobbit door to the deck, the homemade pendant lights in the sitting area, and the built-in cigar humidor all help knock it out of the park. Brian, a former cigar dealer, even repurposed wooden cigar boxes into bookshelves and microcabinets in this home's rear-situated bathroom. The stairs (with storage beneath) are positioned so that they become makeshift seating when the guest list grows. During one of my visits we had seven people sitting comfortably in the living room.

The view from the loft windows is impressive.

DEEK'S TAKEAWAYS

While the headroom in the kitchen is a mere 6 foot, 1 inch or so (tough on some), the trade-off is in a loft. (Furthermore, Brian built the house to fit his own height and needs, so taller visitors just have to deal.) The "extra" loft space makes it easy to maneuver and position oneself before getting into the bed, and it allows ample room for a nightstand, for getting dressed, and for easy access to the roof deck's door.

I'm also a fan of the numerous windows placed to maximize the view (and what a view it is!), not to mention airflow in the hot Tennessee summers. I might advocate for a bigger built-in couch (a small wrap-around), but it would impinge on the large slider entrance and thereby chop off a bit of the majestic vista. There's always a trade-off when dealing with such small spaces, but in the grand scheme of things, Brian has done a fantastic job, and this rental compound is well worth a visit or three.

Hobbit door to deck

Tiny cigar-box cabinet

THE SHANGRI-LITTLE STATS

DIMENSIONS: 24' long × 8' wide × 13'6" tall

SQUARE FOOTAGE: Main area: 192; loft: 80

BUDGET: $50,000

HEATING/COOLING: Klimaire mini split

BATHROOM: Flush toilet to septic; shower

POWER: RV cord hookup

HOT WATER: Rinnai tankless electric water heater

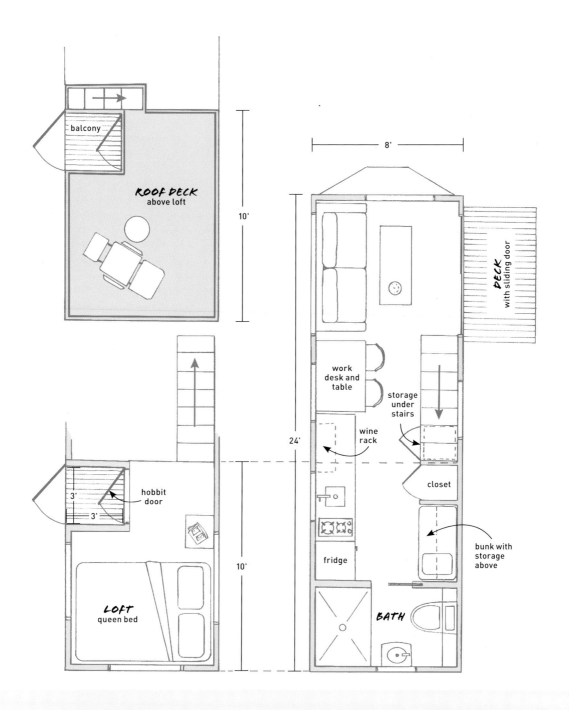

balcony

ROOF DECK
above loft

8'

10'

DECK
with sliding door

24'

work
desk and
table

storage
under
stairs

wine
rack

closet

3'

3'

hobbit
door

bunk with
storage
above

fridge

10'

LOFT
queen bed

BATH

IN RETROSPECT: "If I could go back, I would have designed it with more outdoor outlets and a covered front door. I always thought it would be pretty awesome to take one of the pneumatic messenger tubes from the bank and use it to deliver cold beverages from the kitchen to the rooftop deck. Other than that, the many hours of design paid off, and I am very happy with it."

A cozy sleep cave is tucked beneath the living room "deck."

IQ Container

AUCKLAND, NEW ZEALAND

DESIGN: IQ Containers with Brenda Kelly

I'M A FAN BOY when it comes to shipping container houses. They're cost-effective and they're watertight from the get-go, ready to be retrofitted with insulation and other elements. Of course, step one is to ensure you buy a good, waterproof, used shipping container. Take your time looking around, as these boxes have risen in popularity, along with their prices. Container houses are not for everyone — some people absolutely hate the plain, industrial, modern look of these Conex boxes. But it's important to note that the exteriors can be altered, decorated, or hidden behind other materials.

Brenda Kelly's off-grid New Zealand container house is a case of ultra-tiny gone right. There are a few tricks to her seemingly simple trade. First, light colors were employed to give her microhome an increased sense of openness. It also helps that she was able to procure a slightly taller shipping container (almost 10 feet, as opposed to the usual 8). This extra headroom allowed Brenda to create a two-level design where the sleep space is actually situated below the "living room deck." Usually it's the other way around, but I'm fully in agreement with Brenda's reasoning: "Sleep space isn't for standing." By dropping her bed below and creating a cozy sleep cave, she has omitted the danger of loft ladders and created a space that will please even those who prefer not a sliver of light at night.

DEEK'S TAKEAWAYS

At only 20 feet long, this home is small enough in square footage not to need a building permit, and because of the taller container size, Brenda was able to stack her layout to increase her living space. Building up can be a good solution as long as it's done within reason and not at the cost of open visual space.

As for the downside, due to local restrictions, a space this small can't have an indoor kitchen. Brenda's solution is a grill and a gas burner that she uses outdoors. This would be a big "no" for many people, and a bigger problem in cold climates, but in New Zealand it's a rather workable, even enjoyable, setup. Another disadvantage of an outdoor cook space, though, would be insects — the blood-sucking kind.

Brenda's bathroom, which opens onto the deck, is not part of the main container. Her aim was to keep one's, er, "business" away from the tiny, enclosed living space. While incredibly small, this bathroom employs what I call "clear roof trickery" to fake spaciousness.

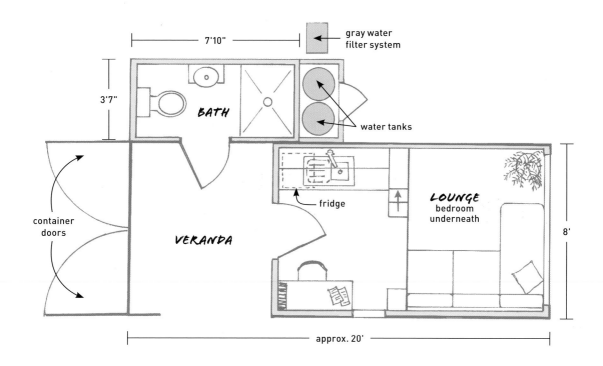

Floor plan labels:
- 7'10"
- gray water filter system
- 3'7"
- BATH
- water tanks
- container doors
- fridge
- LOUNGE — bedroom underneath
- 8'
- VERANDA
- approx. 20'

IQ CONTAINER STATS

DIMENSIONS: 20' long × 8' wide × 10' tall

SQUARE FOOTAGE: 160, plus about 40 with the external bathroom and foyer area

BUDGET: $84,000

HEATING/COOLING: 4-kilowatt (electric) heat pump; natural ventilation for cooling

BATHROOM: Flush toilet to septic; shower

POWER: Grid-tied (net-metered) 2-kilowatt solar-powered system

HOT WATER: Tankless gas water heater

IN RETROSPECT: "I really don't feel I have any regrets, but keep in mind that shipping containers can be tricky to work with because they are tougher to cut and meld to your liking. Insulating them is something you don't want to skimp on, either, as their metallic makeup can be quick to transfer both heat and cold."

Ovida Tiny House

NEAR BOSTON, MASSACHUSETTS

DESIGN:
Addison Godine,
Rachel Moraines,
and Wyatt Komarin

PART OF A SMALL CAMP OF TINY-HOUSE RENTALS of the Getaway House company, the Ovida is as inviting and comfortable as it is ultra-minimal. Reminiscent of pine-clad summer camp cabins, while also giving a nod to the ultra-sparse world of Asian architecture and feng shui, this retreat on wheels is the embodiment of backwoods relaxation.

Like a good many other tiny homes, getaway cabins, and summer destination dwellings, there really isn't much to this space, but that's pretty much the point. The Ovida will bring back sensory memories of the smell of a campfire, the splashing of swimmers from a distant dock, and the clicking of board-game pieces being moved by lantern light. This tiny house really is summer camp, if only for a night or two. And now you get to stay in a cool and cozy little loft rather than the creaky metal bunk beds some of us remember all too well.

Inspiration: "Getaway tiny house designs start from the constraints, including budget, dimensions, and program (what the space will be used for). From there, we chose the idea of a 'modern cabin' to inform the material, finish, and product decisions. The cabins are designed to provide all the comforts of home while emphasizing the natural surroundings."

DEEK'S TAKEAWAYS

The loft is so open and simple that, in this age of overdone sleep spaces, I can't help but love it. It's a space with few distractions, fewer obstructions, and nothing to focus on but the grain of the wood ceiling above and the trees through the windows. I'm not usually a fan of single-tone natural wood interiors, as to me they feel like a one-trick pony that gets winded fast, but this minimal wall work catches the light of the surrounding forest really well. The timber hue is soothing and mesmerizing, and because of the gloss coating, the walls can easily be wiped clean. At the same time, if this look isn't for you, a quick coat of paint could completely alter the feel of the room.

As for storage, there isn't much, as this is truly a minimalist's space, but that could be remedied easily enough with some simple cabinets and shelves and perhaps one or two storage trunks that could double as seating.

OVIDA TINY HOUSE STATS

DIMENSIONS: 20' long × 8'6" wide × 13'6" tall

SQUARE FOOTAGE: Main area: 170; loft: 50

BUDGET: $40,000

HEATING/COOLING: LG heat pump

BATHROOM: Dry Flush waterless toilet (bagged and disposed of after 15 "flushes"); shower

POWER: Grid-tied (30 amp)

HOT WATER: Electric water heater

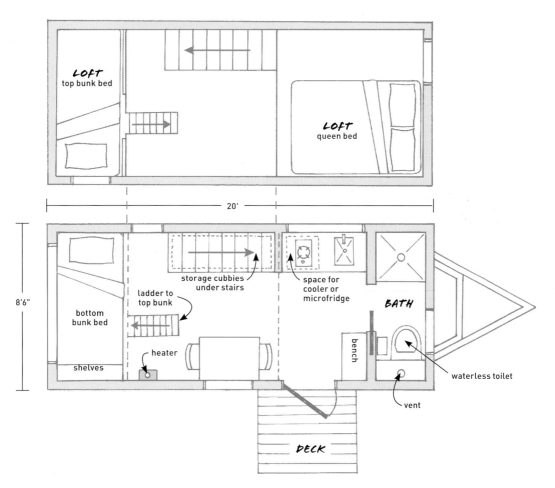

LOFT
top bunk bed

LOFT
queen bed

20'

8'6"

storage cubbies
under stairs

space for
cooler or
microfridge

ladder to
top bunk

BATH

bottom
bunk bed

bench

heater

shelves

waterless toilet

vent

DECK

IN RETROSPECT: "I'd like more headroom in the loft and more counter space."

Jewel's Tiny House

CHARLOTTE,
NORTH CAROLINA

DESIGN:
Jewel Pearson,
Dawn White,
and Jamie Lawson

JEWEL PEARSON (a.k.a. Ms. Gypsy Soul) knew exactly what she wanted, and she designed her life space around her particular needs, wants, and style. Sense a pattern here? This is one of the more windowed homes on wheels, laid out to take in the landscape. I might be beating a dead horse, but I'll say it again: having a number of large windows is a surefire way to enhance a space and make it feel less crushingly minuscule. It's a fine line, though, because having too many windows greatly reduces the rigidity of a house, something to be careful of if you are taking it on the road. You could also end up with excessive solar gain and an utter lack of privacy. Jewel, however, seems to have found the right balance.

With a house well under 400 square feet (including its lofts), Jewel used every trick she could get her hands on. She applied light colors (while not shying away from daring pops of red) and kept the floor plan open. The very large circular window doesn't hurt, either, and is a great focal point in the home.

Inspiration: "Macy Miller's build story and blog."

127

A sliding door opens to a very functional bathroom.

The screened-in porch is a tiny house luxury.

DEEK'S TAKEAWAYS

The giant ocular window steals the show, but Jewel's sense of style and color doesn't hurt one bit! The add-on, 4-foot-deep screened porch is both attractive and original, particularly since it serves as the base of a balcony that Jewel can access from her main sleep loft. This home has two lofts, I might add, which would be very convenient for guests, or for storage when she's flying solo. One simple note of caution (again) is that vertical loft ladders are awkward to ascend, so if it were my place, I might contemplate changing the access to the secondary loft.

Sure, a giant circular window might cost a small fortune, but if you're designing your own custom-fit dream home, as Jewel was, why not splurge here and there?

Pipe ladder

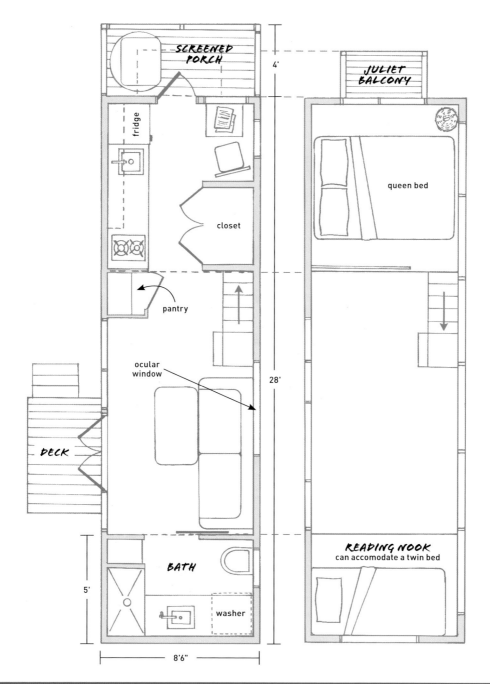

SCREENED PORCH

JULIET BALCONY

fridge

closet

queen bed

pantry

ocular window

DECK

28'

4'

READING NOOK
can accomodate a twin bed

BATH

5'

washer

8'6"

JEWEL'S TINY HOUSE STATS

DIMENSIONS: 28' long × 8'6" wide × 13'6" high, plus a 4' screened-in porch

SQUARE FOOTAGE: Main area: 240; lofts (total): 120

BUDGET: $85,000

HEATING/COOLING: Mini split system and Envi heaters

BATHROOM: Macerating toilet; shower

POWER: Grid-tied

HOT WATER: Tankless electric water heater

The sliding window in Jewel's main sleep loft opens onto a mini balcony.

IN RETROSPECT: "I would have built with more self-confidence had I known how truly perfect my design was for me and how much I'd love my house."

Inspiration:
"The Morrison's 'hOMe' tiny house model/design."

The Empty Nest

PORTLAND, OREGON

DESIGN:
Michelle Boyle

WHILE I FEEL I'VE ALMOST OVER-COVERED the wheeled version of tiny housing, it also seems that some of the best examples of truly tiny homes are in mobile form. Michelle Boyle's Empty Nest is no exception, and it sports one of the nicer, more realistic kitchens I've seen in some time. The notion of "living tiny" may be frequently rooted in thrift, but there's nothing wrong with spending a little extra on some select high-end elements. In Michelle's home it would be her matching vintage kitchen appliances. Yes, these items took a long time to track down, and they cost more than their modern counterparts, but the look and effect are great and, more importantly, just what Michelle wanted. And that's really what the self-designed home is all about, isn't it? Building and creating what suits *you*.

While not extravagant, the Empty Nest doesn't cheap out in other areas, either. The dual lofts, with ample room for both storage and sleeping space, are well worth the time and lumber. The high-backed stuffed chairs look inviting and comfortable. And it's the little touches that make the difference: the small eye-candy appeal of license-plate siding, the lighting, the reclaimed barn wood on the walls, and the classy kitchen tile work on the backsplash all add to Boyle's kettle of coolness.

These hollow stairs double as storage cubbies.

I'm clearly a fan of this home, but the jury may be out regarding the placement of the bathroom. Some argue that a bathroom, for layout and plumbing efficiency (less tubing, pipe, and drain lines), should back up against a kitchen wall, while others believe that it should be as far away from the kitchen as possible, arguing that food prep and food, er, "disposal" make for awkward bedfellows. For the sake of savings I tend to side with the less-plumbing folks. However, Michelle's design — placing the bathroom at the opposite end of the house from the kitchen — does work and flow well.

Window ledges serve as a railing to hold while climbing the stairs.

The bathroom includes a composting toilet.

IN RETROSPECT: "I don't really regret anything, but transitioning into such a small space was a psychological challenge, since I now live alone for the first time in 20 years. Solitude is both a liberating and intimidating new reality."

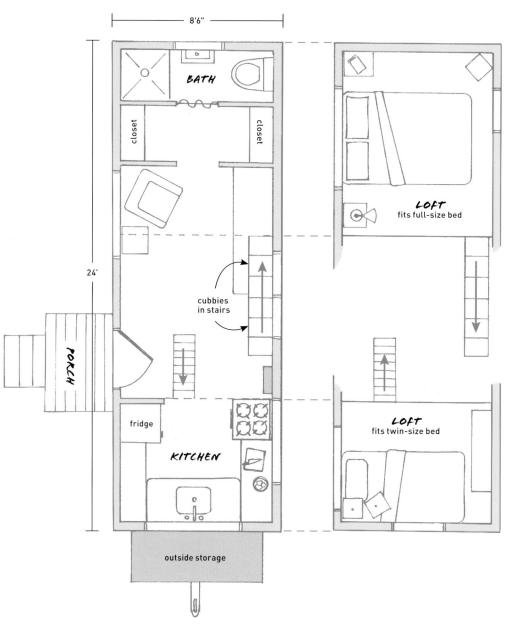

8'6"

24'

BATH

closet

closet

PORCH

cubbies
in stairs

fridge

KITCHEN

outside storage

LOFT
fits full-size bed

LOFT
fits twin-size bed

THE EMPTY NEST STATS

DIMENSIONS: 24' long × 8'6" wide × 13'6" tall

SQUARE FOOTAGE: Main area: 204;
lofts (total): 180

BUDGET: $35,000

HEATING/COOLING: 14,000 Btu in-wall,
vented propane heater

TOILET: Nature's Head composting toilet;
shower

POWER: Grid-tied (20 amp)

HOT WATER: Tankless propane water heater

Real-World Tips for Tiny Kitchen Survival

MICHELLE BOYLE

Whether you're a creative chef type or prefer take-out, you'll likely need a kitchen in your tiny house. If you have a full-size house, your appliance collection is pretty standard: a four-burner stove with an oven, and a refrigerator. Even if you never use them, you have them. In a tiny house, space is at a premium, so your decisions about what you include and what you omit become very important. And whether you finally settle on a galley-style,

L-shaped, or U-shaped kitchen, making the most of this frequently used space will likely mean the difference between loving and hating your tiny home.

But where to start? How to decide?

During the 15 months it took me to build mine, and since, I have learned so much about tiny house living and space utilization. I made mistakes, sure, but hopefully you won't have to make the same ones.

So, without further ado, here is my tiny house kitchen advice.

LAYOUT AND DESIGN. Nowhere is layout more important in a tiny house than in the kitchen. Knowing your own cooking and entertaining habits will be the key to your sanity and success. If your prep space is too small, you'll end up constantly moving around ingredients and dirty dishes. If your floor space is too small for the number of cooks in your kitchen, one bump between butts could lead to spilt milk or, worse, a knife dropping on your foot!

NOT TOO BIG, NOT TOO SMALL, BUT JUUUST RIGHT. If you're not a self-described "culinary enthusiast" and/or cannot remember the last time you cooked for anyone but yourself, you can probably get by with a single-burner countertop stove, no oven, and a dorm-size refrigerator. If you're going to be cooking for two, you should consider at least two burners and a midsize refrigerator. But if you'll be cooking for more than a couple of people or love the flexibility that a full-size kitchen will provide, pencil one in! There's no need to sacrifice your passion for food while living in a tiny house.

CUPBOARDS OR SHELVES. A good way to keep your kitchen area open but also have plenty of storage is to use shelves instead of upper cabinets. And, in keeping with the everything-should-have-more-than-one-purpose mantra, your dishes can easily serve as colorful decor. Using shelves also forces you to monitor your storage and dish-cleaning habits in real time instead of allowing you to shove whatever wherever and close the door. If, however, out-of-sight-out-of-mind is your goal, cabinets are your pal (assuming you have also considered their additional weight).

GARBAGE AND COMPOST. When cooking, the one thing you'll access more than your refrigerator is your garbage can and/or compost bin. And, since floor space is at a premium in tiny kitchens, you'll need to plan for a very handy and accessible area for them both. For instance, a space under the countertop will fit the bill. I have a curtain that I can pull back when I'm cooking, and when I'm done, I close it and don't have to see the ugly, gray 30-gallon can (and neither do my guests).

> Nowhere is layout more important in a tiny house than in the kitchen.

CANS, BOXES, AND FRESH FOOD. Tiny house enthusiasts are well known for their passion for all things environmentally responsible. When planning your trip to the grocery store or farmers' market, have a mental picture of your tiny food storage area to help keep you from overbuying. The less food you buy, the less likely you'll have to throw some out before you consume it. And besides, fresh food is just so much better. I've found that having a tiny kitchen has made me more intentional about what I buy. My advice: buy fresh, buy often, and consume canned goods rarely and boxed foods even less.

CLEANING AND SANITATION. You don't need chemicals to clean your tiny kitchen. Very hot water and sulfate-free soaps are your sanitation friends! To avoid attracting little pests, clear your countertops once a month and clean under and behind every nook and cranny and countertop appliance.

UTENSILS. Your grandmother, and likely your mother, has at least three of every single kitchen utensil imaginable. And while a garlic press is pretty handy, you can peel and chop a clove just as easily with a paring knife. You don't need six spatulas, because you'll be washing dishes as you go. Right? Keeping utensils in a countertop crock or bin is a great way to ensure that you won't keep more than you need. No cheating by sticking them in the drawer!

POTS AND PANS. Vertical storage is your best asset in a tiny house. Don't waste your precious drawers, cupboards, or cubbies by storing pots and pans in them. Besides, ergonomically, accessing pots and pans hung near to the stove is so much easier. No bending or risking a bumped head on your way back up from under the countertop. And, if you're washing your pots and pans with very hot water, you can just hang them to dry, right where they're stored. I love my pot rack!

PRIORITIZE YOUR SPACE. If you have a chance to help design your tiny house, you totally should do it. I have dedicated shelf and display space for my wine collection, glasses, and liquor. I don't imagine everyone would, but I love entertaining, and my kitchen practically says "welcome" to

all my guests when they see my vertical bar! If you love to bake or brew or can or ferment or grow, prioritize your tiny house kitchen space accordingly. You probably won't have enough space for every kitchen gadget and bakeware piece from your grandma, so make the most of what you have by being clear about what you're most passionate about.

Tiny houses aren't for everyone. And isn't that the point? But if you've chosen this path, and you're looking for an intentional lifestyle full of creative space and freedom, then you've come to the right movement! Tiny kitchens aren't for everyone, either. And even though my 8 × 9-foot kitchen is considered huge by tiny house standards, it did require a plan to maximize every square inch.

It took me over two years to locate my collection of vintage appliances. I spent months and over a thousand dollars refurbishing them. The tile on my kitchen wall fell off so many times during installation, I had to go to therapy to recover. My countertops had to be cut three times to fit just perfectly. Sourcing my red dish set and little red owl teapot was truly a labor of love. But in the end, my tiny kitchen is my favorite room in my tiny house.

I cook.

I clean.

I entertain.

I'm in tiny house kitchen heaven.

> **If you love to bake or brew or can or ferment or grow, prioritize your tiny house kitchen space accordingly.**

Michelle Boyle's journey to tiny started long ago with her fascination with an old farmhouse that she would ride by on her bike on her way to work. Ever since, she's been sketching floor plans and decorating small, intimate spaces. Her tiny house, aptly named "Empty Nest" (page 133), was her first opportunity to build a space just for her (Michelle is a proud single mom of two college-aged children). She is a published author, accomplished speaker, patented inventor, popular blogger, craigslist stalker, enthusiastic glamper, and the hostess of the **Tiny House Podcast***, as well as a passionate tiny house advocate, designer, builder, and occupant.*

Kyle's Vermont Cabin

HARDWICK, VERMONT

DESIGN: **Kyle Woolard**

ADDING TO THIS COLLECTION'S SIMPLER SHELTERS is another build from one of our workshop attendees. Kyle Woolard, a musician (front man for the band The Anatomy of Frank) and builder, took the rather gutsy risk of purchasing a plot of land leagues away from his Virginia home with the aim of making it a getaway, rental, or eventual full-time landing space. In a rather short time, using locally sourced wood and materials, Kyle was able to take what he had dreamed and scrawled on paper and bring it to life: off-grid, in the woods, by a creek, and all for very little loot.

While it's no micro Taj Mahal (that's the whole point), this is still a very comfortable home, with a woodstove, pallet-wood ceilings, a propane range, and a cozy sleep loft. As for washing, the tiny bathroom space houses a shower crafted from a livestock feeding trough. This is not an uncommon move in the tiny house world, but it's the source of water that isn't so common. Kyle tapped into a flow of water falling from a cliff behind his house, diverted it to his cabin via a pipe, and channeled it into a wall-mounted propane heater. This heater, meant for outdoor use, was installed indoors and then retrofitted with a ducted vent. In the winter, this source of free water is not so free-flowing, so Kyle and guests opt for the simplest option at hand: lugging in their water, heating it in a kettle, filling a spigoted cooler, and hanging that cooler from the ceiling for a short, but hot, shower.

DEEK'S TAKEAWAYS

This might be the only home in this book that uses slab siding. Slab siding planks are the mill's early cuts from a log, and for that reason they are less clean, less square, and, to most, less desirable. However, live-edge plank siding is also less expensive — far less expensive. Some mills even give this wood away, or come close to it. The look is very backwoods and can come off attractively in its simplicity.

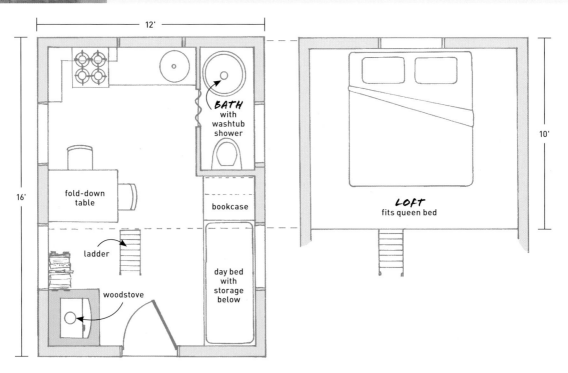

Check out the burlap coffee sacks on the cabinets. Whether you like the look or not, they are cheap, take little time to make, and don't require swing space, unlike "proper" cabinet doors.

KYLE'S VERMONT CABIN STATS

DIMENSIONS: 16' long × 12' wide × 14' tall

SQUARE FOOTAGE: Main area: 165; loft: 80

BUDGET: Around $15,000

HEATING/COOLING: Jotul woodstove

BATHROOM: Homemade bucket-style composting toilet; feeding trough shower

POWER: None; generator for tool use

HOT WATER: Tankless propane water heater; heated in kettles on a range in winter

IN RETROSPECT: "I don't have any real regrets, but every time I see the house, I find myself in a state of complete awe that we built it all without a driveway. Every screw, every bag of concrete, and every single tool, board, and piece of hardware had to be hauled across a stream, up a rocky hill, and to the site. I don't regret it, I just wouldn't be crazy enough to do it a second time."

The space behind the stairs is a storage closet. The steps could be filled in to better hide it.

The Bunkaboose

**COLORADO SPRINGS,
COLORADO**

DESIGN:
David Papen and Darin Zaruba
of Omega Modular Group
(Joplin, Missouri)

DARIN ZARUBA has to be one of the busier guys in the tiny home field. Aside from once being the full-time big cheese behind his Colorado Springs–based company, Eco Cabins, he was also the catalyst, the keystone, and the sleepless energy behind the epic small-living festival Tiny House Jamboree. As a testament to the growth in interest in tiny homes, in 2016, "THE Jamboree," as it's known, brought in no fewer than 50,000 heads in just two days. And this is where I first stumbled upon Darin's Bunkaboose model.

For those nervous about the prospect of going tiny, the 24-foot Bunkaboose is no sacrificial affair. The design includes not only a full refrigerator but also a wine fridge, a microwave, an induction range, and, well, just about anything a cooking geek might desire. Further rounding out the luxury of this home, there are two lofts (one with a king-size bed), an electric fireplace, storage-stairs, a closet, and a "presidential porch" (à la the caboose decks where presidents of old gave whistle-stop speeches). Mr. Z doesn't mess around.

Inspiration: "We [Darin and David] both like old stuff and rust. Old machines and buildings. The inspiration was an old caboose where presidents did stump speeches from the back railing as they traveled the country — it's why we included the rear posted deck on this model."

DEEK'S TAKEAWAYS

I love the use of pipe fittings as railings and holds and have done it myself in tree house and tiny house work. It's affordable, strong as all heck, and easy to do, and it broadcasts an industrial-modern look (or rustic-industrial, in this case). The porch is another great aspect of this build, although some might see it as a waste of trailer deck space, given that you're on wheels. The only change I might make would be to add skylights or some other way to get airflow and light into the king-size bed loft. Light and ventilation, never mind egress, are something to keep in mind with any design.

"Rustic-industrial is kind of our style," says Zaruba.

A Galvalume-lined shower was a fan favorite at the Jamboree, as was the water closet — a separate little room for the toilet and stackable washer-dryer unit.

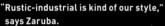

The tongue-and-groove paneling from beetle kill pine is a great example of salvaged material that also serves a decorative purpose. It adds visual appeal even without having much wall art.

IN RETROSPECT:
"We would have gone with a lower, movable loft and made the storage loft over the kitchen big enough for a double bed."

An electric fireplace, induction range, and full-size fridge make it clear this house is not about sacrifice.

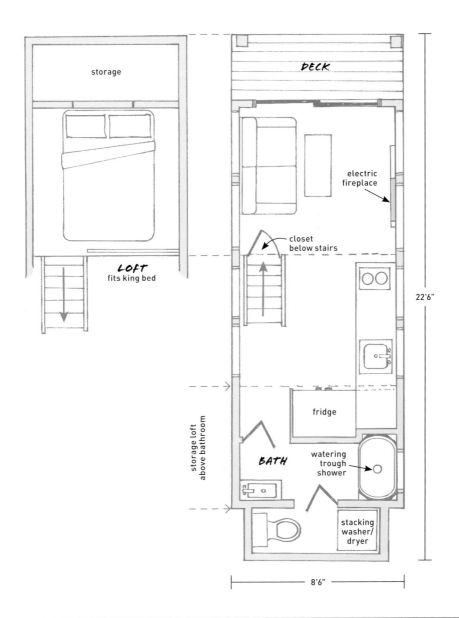

storage

DECK

electric
fireplace

closet
below stairs

LOFT
fits king bed

22'6"

storage loft
above bathroom

fridge

BATH

watering
trough
shower

stacking
washer/
dryer

8'6"

THE BUNKABOOSE STATS

DIMENSIONS: 22'6" long × 8'6" wide ×
13'6" tall

SQUARE FOOTAGE: Main area: 218
(not counting the front deck); loft: 100
(it goes over the deck)

BUDGET: $59,000 retail

HEATING/COOLING: Mitsubishi mini split

BATHROOM: Standard flush toilet; shower

POWER: RV cord hookup (50-amp)

HOT WATER: Tankless electric water heater

ATL Shipping Container Home

ATLANTA, GEORGIA

DESIGN:
Gabriel Beckman, owner,
Bolder Container Homes;
interior design by
Adele Taylor Ulrich
and Gabriel Beckman

THIS INDUSTRIAL-MODERN SHIPPING CONTAINER home stands as solid, metallic proof of how much you can do with an 8 × 20-foot box. While shipping containers are limited in size and shape, there are seemingly endless ways to configure them, pretty 'em up, and give them new life. You can also get creative by combining and stacking them. Often decommissioned after a short life in harbor freight, these giant lunchbox-like vessels are reasonably inexpensive and give you a fully enclosed and dry space to work with from the get-go.

In this case, right smack in the middle of a culturally diverse and artsy district of Atlanta lies something like an urban homestead run by Adele Ulrich and Ray Manlove. As with many shipping container conversions, there's more here than first meets the eye. What looks stark and simple from the outside turns out to be a rather big and pleasant surprise on the inside. The glass double doors bring in light, create the illusion of space, and prevent you from feeling like you're being shoehorned into the entryway. Add in a spacious bathroom (rare in container conversions), both sleep and relaxation spaces, and an abundance of fun, daring, and gorgeous artisan decor pieces (many procured locally and from Etsy), and there's little left to be desired here.

The wood shipping container headboard was love at first sight for me. Best of all, it was found as-is and merely cut to size.

DEEK'S TAKEAWAYS

The sparse yet daring decor and color scheme make this place one of my favorites. I also love the bed: it's built with recessed supports and appears to hover above the floor, especially when lighted from below by the LED lights. The clever design achieves a unique and modern look and creates a stow space for suitcases or clothing baskets, all out of kicking range. Finally, I appreciate the simplicity of the floor itself — just the plywood original, with some sanding and stain.

The drawbacks of shipping container homes include the difficulty of insulating them and the chore of cutting through thick steel to make way for windows and doors. But as you can see, it can be done, and done well. It's also tough to make them not look so industrial and boxy — if that's a look you aren't so keen on. However, if you're willing to think outside the box (pun intended), it is possible to gussy 'em up and even hide the fact that there is a mere container at the core.

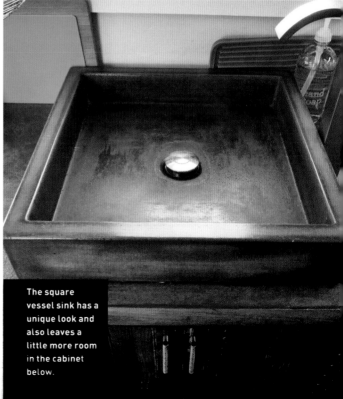

A fold-down breakfast bar allows for a kitchen seating.

The square vessel sink has a unique look and also leaves a little more room in the cabinet below.

Inspiration: "Gabriel had been watching the repurposing of shipping containers online for some time. With the widening of the Port of Savannah, the time seemed right to start taking shipping containers that were no longer crossing the ocean and recycle them into living spaces. Adele had been working to raise awareness about green consumerism for decades, along with other social justice issues and using the arts as a means to reach people. Voluntary simplicity is a place where design and green living intersect. Adele first fell in love with the idea of refurbishing shipping containers by reading eco-design books. With the help of her partner, Ray Manlove, this all became a reality."

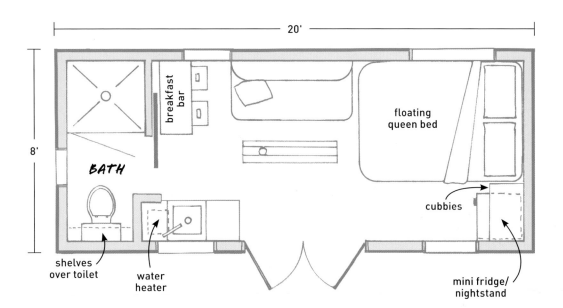

20'

8'

breakfast bar

floating queen bed

cubbies

BATH

shelves over toilet

water heater

mini fridge/ nightstand

ATL SHIPPING CONTAINER HOME STATS

DIMENSIONS: 20' long × 8' wide × 8' tall

SQUARE FOOTAGE: 160

BUDGET: $65,000

HEATING/COOLING: Air-Con mini split

BATHROOM: Flush toilet to septic; shower

POWER: Grid-tied (60 amp)

HOT WATER: Rheem tankless electric water heater

IN RETROSPECT: "I would have made the awnings about 8 inches deeper. I love how they look, but they are a bit tight in a heavy rain."

The Maiden Mansion

SEATTLE, WASHINGTON

DESIGN:
Hannah Rose Crabtree
(her tiny house company
is called Pocket Mansions)

Inspiration:
"This house, though
I built it for myself,
was designed for an
imaginary woman.
I wanted the house
to have everything
her main house had
without having to
sacrifice anything. It
was a design challenge
to include so much in
such a small space."

HANNAH CRABTREE DREAMED of creating her own custom tiny house — not one from stock plans but rather a home that would suit her personal needs, tastes, and style. All it takes is a glimpse into her domain to see that she got what she gunned for. Having spent a night in this house on my last book tour (she also rents it out), I can attest that, unlike some other homes that are "more looks than logic," this little space really works well for comfortable living. It also has more storage space than almost any other tiny house in this book.

Hannah's home falls into the category of "luxury tiny house," what with the cedar shingles, gel-fuel fireplace, wall of windows, washer-dryer combo, butane range, and even a convection oven. While not all of those are necessarily pricey items, comfortably fitting them into a small space is a tricky science that Hannah seems to have mastered.

The stars of the Maiden Mansion have to be transformation and hidden storage. The L-shaped seating by the entrance transforms into a bed or breaks apart to accommodate a dining table that drops down from the wall. As for storage, you'll find kickspace storage beneath the cabinets, slide-out drawers in the pantry, and even a long, thin, multitiered shelving unit on a track that hides in a small gap next to her refrigerator.

Proponents of ultra-minimalism might say that Hannah put too much in this small space. I love it, though, for how it fits the owner's personality and interests, and because there's a little something clever to be found at every turn. For instance, the laundry hatch built into the top riser of the loft steps isn't all that time-saving or practical, but it is fun — and that certainly counts. I'm also a fan of the mini "shed" attached to the back of the home (for the electrical panel, water heater, and additional storage). The kitchen counter that becomes 7 feet long with the help of a small flip-up table makes for a very workable kitchen. The USB outlets are a nice little touch, too.

Flip-up counter

The wall of windows on the gable end opens up the space visually and helps vent the loft.

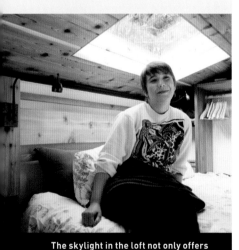

The skylight in the loft not only offers a view of the swaying trees above but also increases the bed's sitting height, making even the tallest people less apt to bump their heads.

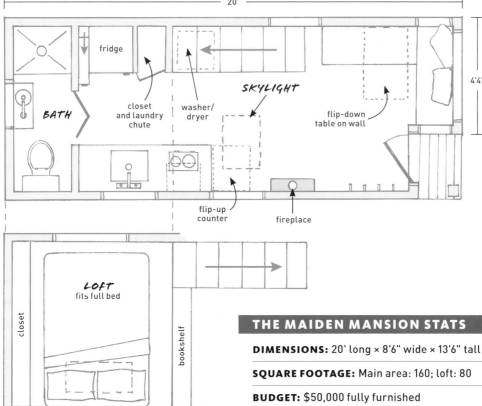

20'

fridge

SKYLIGHT

BATH

closet and laundry chute

washer/ dryer

flip-down table on wall

4'4"

8'6"

flip-up counter

fireplace

LOFT
fits full bed

closet

bookshelf

THE MAIDEN MANSION STATS

DIMENSIONS: 20' long × 8'6" wide × 13'6" tall

SQUARE FOOTAGE: Main area: 160; loft: 80

BUDGET: $50,000 fully furnished

HEATING/COOLING: Electric kickspace heater under kitchen cabinet; AC window unit for summer

BATHROOM: Compact flush toilet (originally a Nature's Head composting toilet, but guests could not handle its operation); shower

POWER: Grid-tied (house is wired for 60 amps but runs on two 20-amp circuits)

HOT WATER: Rinnai V53eP tankless propane water heater

IN RETROSPECT: "The dining table should have been recessed into the wall so as not to cause the couch to bump out. I also would've run my plumbing inside and left it exposed so it didn't all freeze on me. And I would've used the Separett composting toilet from the get-go as it's extremely user-friendly. Dealing with a blackwater tank is a nightmare."

Hannah's sense of style comes out in the details, as with the elegant bathroom sink and golden decor.

Minimalism: Getting It, and Getting There

RYAN NICODEMUS

The thought of living in a tiny home is a daydream to get lost in. Imagine yourself residing on a piece of land with wooded trails and mountains filling the backyard view. There's a beautiful green lawn with a fire pit, comfy outdoor chairs, a picnic table, and plenty of room for your 300-square-foot home.

It's morning, and as the sun rises over the mountains and the light hits your eyelids, a few birds start chirping, and you're awakened by the gentle harmony of nature. You get out of your loft bed and climb down an oak ladder crafted from a tree that fell in the forest behind your home. As you're grinding fresh coffee, you notice three robins outside your kitchen window bathing in the birdbath carved from the same oak. Steaming cup of coffee in hand, you grab a well-worn book, step out onto the porch, and ease into a rocking chair. You sip your coffee, turning pages without distraction. There's peace and quiet, both physically and mentally: no mortgage to worry about, no debt looming over your head. Your biggest decision that day is deciding whether you're going to finish your book in the evening or try to capture the sunset on canvas.

For some this sounds like the perfect life — but how do you get there? Uprooting yourself and moving into a tiny home doesn't happen overnight, especially if you live with other people. So how do you prepare for life in a tiny home? Many people have looked toward a lifestyle known as minimalism as a way to help.

Don't worry — minimalism doesn't mean you have to rent a dumpster and throw out all your stuff. It doesn't mean you have to rid yourself of art and let go of all the physical books you own. Getting rid of stuff is not the point. You see, minimalism is the thing that gets us past the things so we can make room for life's import-ant things — which actually aren't things at all. Minimalism helps us determine what is essential in our lives. When moving into a tiny home, it's important, and necessary, to bring with you only the things that serve a purpose or bring you joy. Everything else is superfluous.

Before I made minimalism part of my life, I had no idea what was important. I spent years working 60-, 70-, sometimes 80-hour weeks. I did this so I could afford a brand-new car every couple of years. I did this so I could pay for my 2,000-square-foot home with three bedrooms, two

bathrooms, and two living rooms (yes, two living rooms!). I was living the American Dream. I consumed as much as I could simply because I had the means to afford all those debt payments. I was the perfect consumer, trapped in a lifestyle that forced me to keep putting in the long hours to maintain my consumption habits. Money in, money out. It was a vicious cycle.

I became aware of minimalism thanks to my best friend, Joshua Fields Millburn. He and I worked side-by-side at the same corporation, for the same grumpy boss, in the same crummy work environment, for the same awful amount of years. We were miserable — until I noticed Joshua wasn't anymore. He was making changes in his life that I didn't fully understand.

When he moved into a new apart-ment, it came with a TV mount on the wall, ready for a big screen. I anticipated what kind of TV he was going to buy — how big, what brand? But then months passed and he still had no TV, just an empty mount. What was going on?

I noticed Joshua's attitude shift over several months. His shoul-ders were more relaxed. His face expressed less angst. The blistering words our boss spewed at us during meetings seemed to roll off his back. So I took him to lunch and asked him

> **Bring with you only the things that serve a purpose or bring you joy. Everything else is superfluous.**

why he was so damn happy. I thought maybe the doctor had prescribed him some highly effective antidepressants. But that wasn't it at all: Joshua had started living intentionally. He explained how he had discovered a lifestyle called minimalism, which helped him clear the clutter from his life to make room for what was most important. After listening to his story, minimalism started to make sense to me — it became an attractive solution to my growing disillusionment. I realized that if I was willing to let go of my big home, new car, and compulsory consumption, I wouldn't need to earn that six-figure salary, and therefore wouldn't need to work those crazy hours.

How might my life be better with less?

When I decided to become a minimalist, I didn't know where to start — I just knew I wanted to make a change right away. So Joshua and I came up with this crazy idea called a "packing party."

We packed all my belongings as if I were moving, and then I unpacked only the items I needed over the next three weeks. Joshua came over and helped me box up everything: my clothes, my kitchenware, my towels, my electronics, my TVs, my framed photographs and paintings, my toiletries — even my furniture! Everything. We literally pretended I was moving. Then I spent the next 21 days unpacking only the items I

needed. My toothbrush. My bed and bedsheets. Clothes for work. The furniture I actually used. Kitchenware. A tool set. Just the things that added value to my life. After three weeks, 80 percent of my stuff was still sealed in boxes. I looked at those boxes, and I couldn't even remember what was in most of them. All those things that were supposed to make me happy weren't doing their job. So I donated and sold all of it.

This experience was life-altering, and I wanted to share it with the world. I went to Joshua and told him how my perspective had changed, and how this story might be able to help others in a similar situation. So he and I started a website. In the six years since we started TheMinimalists.com, we've gained more than 10 million annual readers, published three books, traveled around the world on a 100-city book tour, and released a feature-length documentary to share our simple-living message.

So how does one begin a journey into minimalism? After all, a packing party may seem a tad extreme for some. A great first step toward practicing minimalism is to ask yourself, How might my life be better with less? Understanding the why behind simplifying will ultimately drive you to take those first steps. For me, the benefits were reclaiming my time and gaining control of my finances. For you, the benefits might be cleaning your home faster, getting out of debt, feeling lighter and freer without a hoard of stuff, worrying less about the upkeep of things, having more time to give to your loved ones, or having the freedom to move into a tiny home. The benefits will be different for everyone.

Now that you understand the benefits, what are some practical action steps? If a packing party isn't your ideal starting point, consider the 30-Day Minimalism Game. Most of us know how boring decluttering can be, so here's how you make it fun: First, find a friend, family member, or co-worker who wants to declutter his or her life, too. Second, pick the month that you want to start (next month is the best month — strike while the iron's hot!). On the first day, each of you must get rid of one thing. On the second, two things. Three items on the third. And so forth. Anything can go! Clothes, furniture, electronics, tools, decorations, etc. Donate, sell, or recycle. Whatever you choose, each possession must be out of your house — and out of your life — by midnight each day. It's an easy game at first. However, it becomes more challenging by week two when you're jettisoning more than a dozen items each day. Whoever can keep it going the longest wins; you both win

if you make it all month because you each will have rid yourselves of about 500 items.

Once you rid yourself of the excess stuff in your life, you can then determine what your needs will be. At The Minimalists blog we write about the three categories our possessions fall into: Needs, Wants, and Likes.

NEEDS. What do you truly need to live? Everyone is different, but most of us have the same basic needs. So what do you need? Food? Shelter? Video games?

WANTS. Many of the things you want can lead to happiness. The problem is that we indulge too many of our Wants — new vehicles, designer clothes, impulse buys — many of which end up being Likes instead of Wants. Ask yourself: What adds value to my life?

LIKES. This category is for when you say things like, "Yeah, I like my satellite radio, but I don't get a ton of value from it." Or "I like that dress, it's soooo my style, but I don't really need any new clothes." It can be hard to notice how many of the things we just sort of like suck up a ton of our income. Purchasing these Likes often feels great in the moment, but the post-purchase high wears off by the time the credit-card statement enters your mailbox. It's an odd double-bind: it turns out you don't really like many of your Likes at all.

Okay, you've made your list, you've got your three categories, and now it's time to take action. We'll start from the bottom and work our way up. (This is what I did before I was ready to make any big life changes.)

> **Your Wants are important — they add value to your life — but they're not more important than changing your life.**

MONTH 1. Get rid of 100 percent of your Likes. All of them — gone.

MONTH 2. Get rid of 100 percent of your Wants. Yes, all of them (at first). Once you've made the necessary changes in your life, you can reintroduce your Wants one at a time — though you'll likely realize you want far fewer of your old Wants (your pacifiers) once you're following a more meaningful path. Your Wants are important — they add value to your life — but they're not more important than changing your life.

MONTH 3. Reduce your Needs by at least 50 percent. More, if you can. You might be thinking: But I need a roof over my head! I need to eat! I need my MTV! Okay, you needn't get rid of everything; you needn't live in a hut and eat only Ramen noodles. But you can significantly reduce your cost of living. Can you sell your home? I sold my home so I could cut that monthly payment for a roof over my head by 75 percent. Can you sell your car and get a cheaper one? I traded in my brand-new car for one that was six years old with no car payment. Can you find ways to reduce your food costs by 50 percent? Most likely. While there isn't a cookie-cutter answer for anyone, you can reduce your expenses and live more deliberately.

This is the high price of pursuing your dreams. Unfortunately, many people aren't willing to pay the price, and so their dreams never become Musts for them. They remain Shoulds, which eventually turn into Wishes, which one day become Never-Going-to-Happens, and that story always has a sad ending. Once you extract yourself from the clutches of money, you'll worry less; and once you get rid of your worries, you'll be able to focus on making any change you want to make — including that dream of moving into a tiny home.

That doesn't mean you should go out and quit your job today. It means you should plan accordingly, and when you're ready, you can make the right decision. Knowing you're no longer trapped by the trappings of your previous lifestyle, you can make an informed decision — one that's not based on fear. Every beautiful change takes time and action; it takes time for a bulb to blossom into a flower, for a caterpillar to evolve into a butterfly. These changes are scary at first (they were terrifying for me). And, although big changes are often simple, they're rarely easy. But nothing worth doing ever is.

No matter how you choose to start your minimalist journey, take it one step at a time. Decide what your first step will be and commit. Commitment means following through with massive action. And massive action means taking steps that move you closer to your goal: living a meaningful life in a tiny home.

Ryan Nicodemus, known to his audience as one-half of The Minimalists, helps more than 20 million people live meaningful lives with less through his website, books, podcast, and documentary. The Minimalists have been featured widely and have spoken at Harvard, Apple, SXSW, and TEDx. Their film, **Minimalism***, was the #1 indie documentary of 2016.*

TEENY TINIES

The Cheer Stand

RIEGELWOOD,
NORTH CAROLINA

DESIGN:
Steven Harrell

THIS NORTH CAROLINA BUDGET build by Steven Harrell is a spin-off on deer stands used for hunting. It has to be the thinnest tiny house or vacation cabin out there. Some will argue that it's not really a tiny house, but aside from its lack of insulation, it contains everything needed for a very simple lifestyle: heat via a tiny woodstove, sleeping space for two, a food prep area and mini sink (which now has a proper drain), and an outhouse. Steven even has plans to grid-tie his camp for electricity.

But why is the Cheer Stand so darn emaciated? Steven chose to construct his getaway cabin at only 4 feet wide to keep everything within easy reach, but also because he's long been a fan of unconventional and bizarre micro-architecture. From one end, the cabin seems almost as small as the outhouse, but step toward its long side and the cabin takes on a whole new look with its 16-foot length. The floor is merely two 8-foot sheets of plywood held over the (sometimes swampy) forest floor by 4×6 pressure-treated posts set several feet into the ground. The posts also serve as wall supports and connections, traveling from below the frost line to the roof of the cabin.

Inspiration: "I mulled for two weeks on what I wanted to put in the woods on my property. I'd think about it each night before I went to sleep and kept reminding myself that it had to be simple, functional, fun, and affordable."

I, like Steven, have an affinity for daring and bizarre cabins. And while the dimensions might seem absurd, there is a lot to be gleaned from this design. For instance, the ladder steps built into the wall save a great deal of space. Keep in mind, however, that non-angled ladders and stairs are more difficult (and dangerous) to climb.

I'm also a fan of the window positioning in the loft. Lofts are often hot dens of near-death if not properly ventilated. Steven nipped this problem in the bud by positioning windows on either side of the top bunk for cross ventilation and also to offer a nice view of the outdoors. After spending the night here during a hands-on workshop we taught on Steven's land, I enjoyed slowly waking to the view of stirring campers preparing breakfast at the fire ring. It was also nice to wake up, period, having not been roasted alive.

The "outhouse" adjacent to the cabin isn't all that traditional in that it has a composting, bucket-based toilet — there is no ground pit beneath.

The large deck adds considerable outdoor living space.

IN RETROSPECT: "One night while having a few drinks with my father and brother, we chose the spot to build it in the pitch dark and just got to work. Later we realized it was the lowest spot on the property and that we really should have gotten to know the site before breaking ground. Clay-rich soil meant water pooling underneath in heavy rains. Luckily, the fix was one or two good loads of dirt. Aside from that, if I did it again I might make it 6 feet wide so that when we get a few guests in the cabin, you wouldn't have to squeeze by one another to get to the other side of the room."

The single burner and sink bowl are minimalist but functional.

Mountain Trail Mix

Woodstove

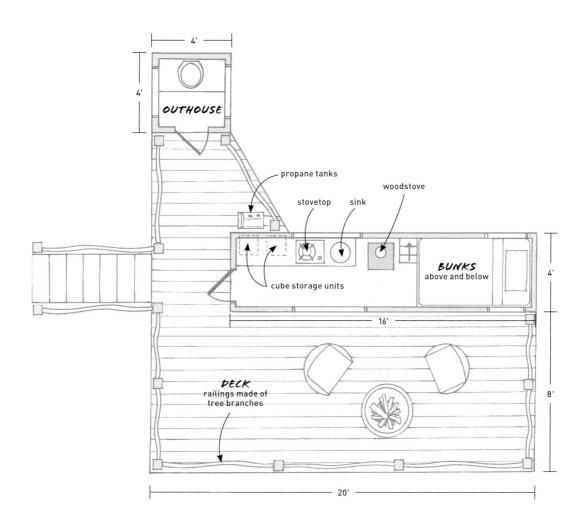

4'

4'

OUTHOUSE

propane tanks

stovetop   sink

woodstove

cube storage units

BUNKS
above and below

4'

16'

DECK
railings made of
tree branches

8'

20'

THE CHEER STAND STATS

DIMENSIONS: 16' long × 4' wide × 10' tall (at peak)

SQUARE FOOTAGE: 64

BUDGET: Around $1,800

HEATING/COOLING: Woodstove
(mini tent-style model); passive cooling

BATHROOM: 4 × 4-foot outhouse attached
to the deck, 5 feet from cabin

POWER: None yet

HOT WATER: Water carried in and heated on a
butane range

The Pallet House

SHREWSBURY,
MASSACHUSETTS

DESIGN:
Joseph Labaire
(remodel and restyling
by Deek Diedricksen)

Inspiration:
"Being broke and
trying not to
spend money
one doesn't have."
—*Joseph*

THIS PALLET HOUSE might take the cake as the most affordable build in this book, since a good portion of it is constructed with free pallet wood. The trade-off, however, is a great deal of time and work, as anyone who has dismantled pallets knows. But this wheeled structure shows that the blisters, board breaking, and back pain might be worth it. With its very DIY, Dr. Seuss–like flavor, it's a good example of how you can suit your own personal budget and style needs.

The Pallet House (or "Pallet Palace," as I like to call it, because it's so UNpalatial) was Joseph Labaire's home for close to a year and served him well as a money-saving alternative to renting an apartment. For that period, his tiny home lay hidden next to an old drive-in theater and directly adjacent to a small sawmill specializing in salvaging downed city trees. Some of those trees became the milled wood that Joseph used when he couldn't find suitable material on the side of the road or in industrial-park alleyways. Beyond the raw charm of the pallets, it only takes a quick look to see just how bare-bones this space is. It's a ramshackle and rustic build, but that's why I love it — and one of the reasons I later bought the house from Joseph when he moved away. It now resides in my backyard as a guest space, an art studio, and a teaching tool for workshop students.

The large built-in shelving unit runs the risk of taking up too much square footage, but it also provides a heck of a lot of stow space.

In the renovation, the old kerosene heater has been replaced by an Envi wall unit. The new ladder takes up less space than the old one.

DEEK'S TAKEAWAYS

I personally might have made the rugged shelves double as steps to the bed, mainly because the loft ladder not only eats up space but also almost rams you into the angled ceiling before you get to the bed's edge. You could move the stepladder farther away from the wall, sure, but then it would eat up the middle of the room. (I didn't end up changing this in the renovation, but I did consider it.) Furthermore, the windows are too small and too widely spaced, and there is not sufficient light in the loft, but I suppose that by having fewer windows, you have more wall space for art and more storage. Fewer windows also means less heat loss (assuming your home is well insulated). This is why you don't often see expansive windows in Alaskan cabins.

I later added a mini reading-nook loft and closed off the bathroom, which was originally just a toilet in the corner. I should add that one thing to keep in mind when laying out a bathroom is to be sure that you have a window worked in, not only for light but also for ventilation. This is especially important if it doubles as a shower cubby, or "wet-bath," as they're known. Also bear in mind that in an extremely small space there will inevitably be some bleeding of moisture and odors from the bathroom (one of the very few incentives to have a detached outhouse).

Joseph in the Pallet House before renovations.

IN RETROSPECT: "Building with pallets took forever! I wouldn't do it again, to be honest. Also, not having an indoor shower and using a camp-style one was adventurous and enjoyable at first, but later when the weather turned colder, it lost its charm. Warm showers are really hard to do without."

—*Joseph*

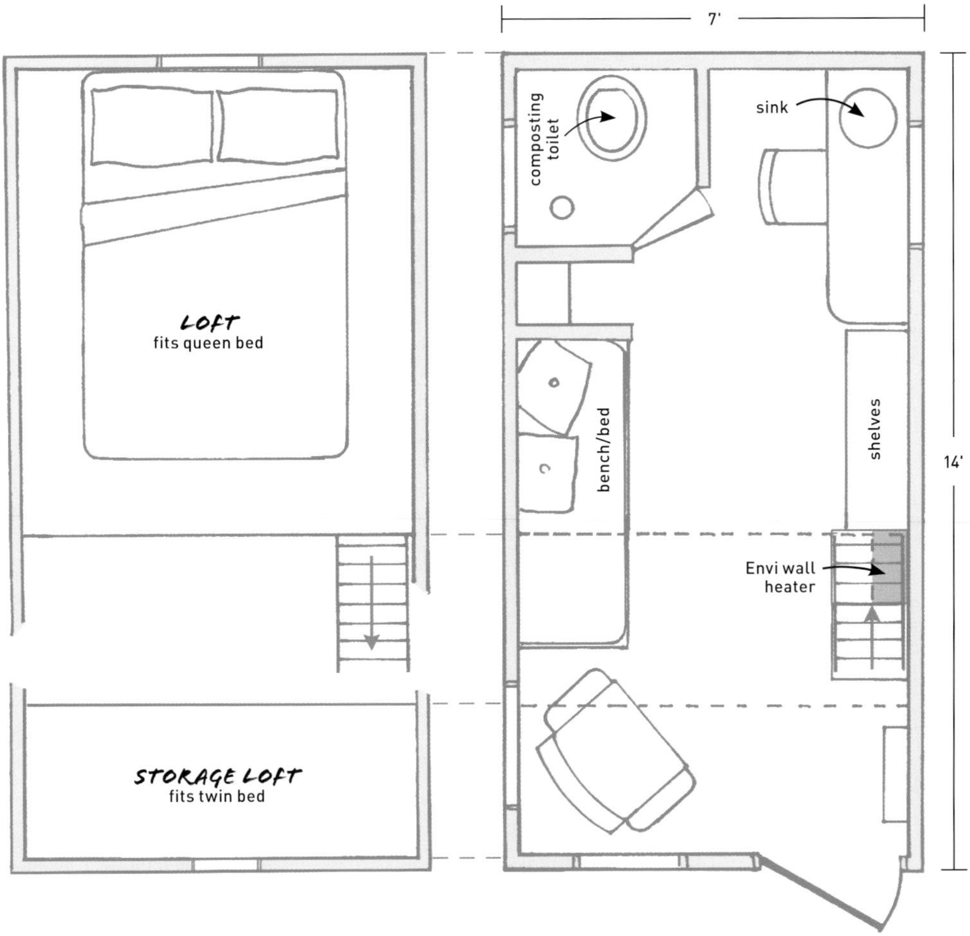
7'
14'
LOFT
fits queen bed
STORAGE LOFT
fits twin bed
composting toilet
sink
bench/bed
shelves
Envi wall heater

THE PALLET HOUSE STATS

DIMENSIONS: 14' long × 7' wide × 11' tall

SQUARE FOOTAGE: Main area: 98; loft: 49

BUDGET: Under $2,000

HEATING/COOLING: Originally a vintage Perfection kerosene heater, currently an Envi wall heater; cooling by a window AC unit when needed

BATHROOM: Composting toilet (wet-bath planned)

POWER: RV cord hookup to grid-tied supply (home nearby)

HOT WATER: Carried in and heated with a butane/propane stove

Eddie's Lego Lair

CLINTON, CONNECTICUT

DESIGN:
Derek "Deek" Diedricksen

EDDIE'S LEGO LAIR may be the smallest structure in this book. Admittedly, it's not a tiny house, but I encourage people to look for inspiration in any microstructure or nontraditional tiny dwellings. Also keep in mind that with the addition of a cook space, more insulation, heat, and a toilet/sink, many small spaces are but a few steps away from being livable tiny houses or vacation cabins.

This modern, towering tree house began with a Make-A-Wish foundation message I received from Eddie's Connecticut family. Eddie requested that I not only design and build this getaway but do some funky graffiti-like art for it as well. How could I say no? When I finally completed Eddie's wish list of tree house "musts," his Lego Lair had its porthole-like window (a reused front-loading washing machine door), a sleep loft (bolstered by old wood from a bed that I had been saving for its second life), a gigantic clear wall made of Tuftex polycarbonate panels, and a deck for hanging out with friends. We even went so far as to bring in a custom Lego table crafted by Bryan Bales. Other notable artists, such as Delaware's Gus Fink, added their framed artwork.

All in all, Eddie's edifice extends 21 feet from the ground to the roof. This structure, I might add, is insulated, with the exception of its south-facing clear front, which allows for passive solar heating in the winter. In the summer the clear wall is shaded by the maple tree the house is attached to, and three windows (one at the highest point) vent this space rather effectively.

The table by Bryan Bales harbors a secret panel and an LED light for display.

★ LIFE IS A GREAT ADVENTURE

DEEK'S TAKEAWAYS

Shingles. With this one it's all about the shingles and, well, color radiance. The Lego Lair is a very simple, albeit unconventional, build, panelized a wall at a time. We never meant it to be fancy, but we did spend the extra time and money to add cedar shingles to three sides. Shingles are a tried-and-true way to add class to an otherwise plain structure.

The building's footprint is 7 feet by 8 feet so that full 8-foot sheets of ¾-inch plywood could be used as roof decking and allow for a nice overhang on the sides. This strategy eliminated the need to add "ladders" (structural eave extenders) to the roof to shed rain and snow. Many often ask, "Why do you frequently make your mini structures such an odd width of 7 feet?" This is why: it all comes down to economy and simplicity.

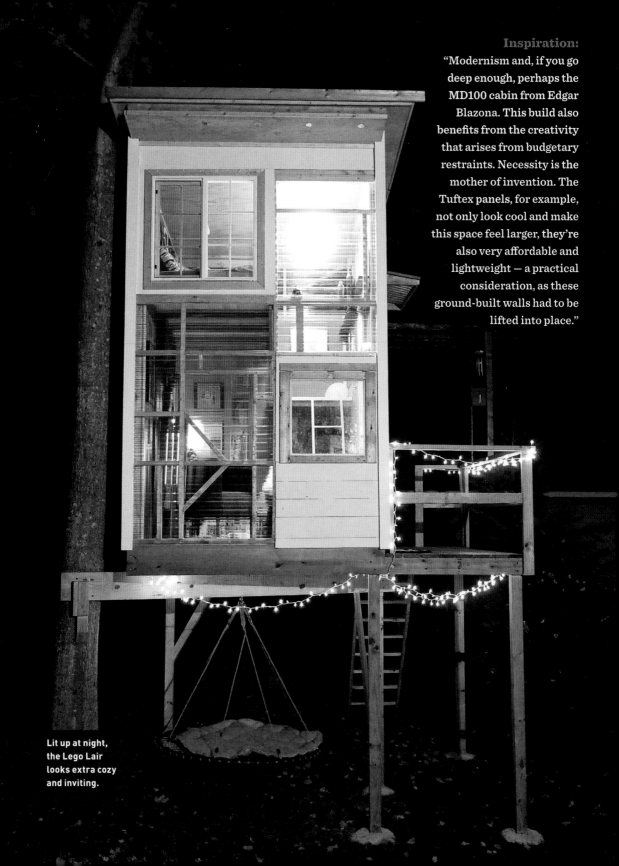

Inspiration: "Modernism and, if you go deep enough, perhaps the MD100 cabin from Edgar Blazona. This build also benefits from the creativity that arises from budgetary restraints. Necessity is the mother of invention. The Tuftex panels, for example, not only look cool and make this space feel larger, they're also very affordable and lightweight — a practical consideration, as these ground-built walls had to be lifted into place."

Lit up at night, the Lego Lair looks extra cozy and inviting.

The loft, with a pipe for a bed rail, makes for a comfy sleep space for one.

IN RETROSPECT:

"While I absolutely love the look of this overall, if it were not for time constraints I would have made this entire tree house a hair bigger. Adding even 2 feet to its length would have made quite a difference. A slightly bigger deck would have been nice as well."

Cliff Cobb of Icarus Lighting created the light-up Lego head.

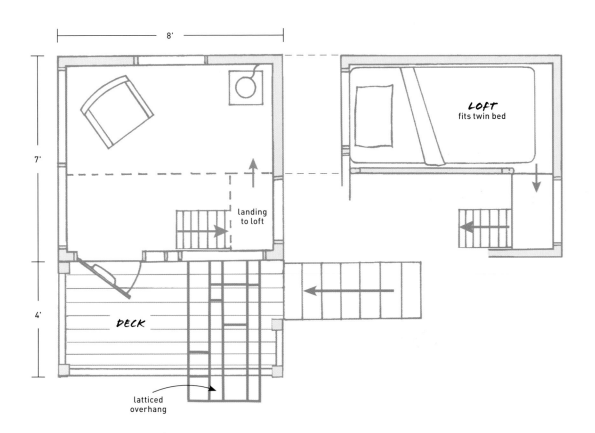

8'

7'

4'

LOFT
fits twin bed

landing
to loft

DECK

latticed
overhang

EDDIE'S LEGO LAIR STATS

DIMENSIONS: 8' long × 7' wide × 10'6" high (interior height); floor is a little over 8' above the ground

SQUARE FOOTAGE: 56

BUDGET: Approximately $3,000 in materials (some reused/salvaged)

HEATING/COOLING: Passive solar, and a plug-in electric heater in the winter

BATHROOM: None (at main house nearby)

POWER: Exterior-grade electrical extension from the nearby house

Andrew's Vardo

LEESBURG, FLORIDA

DESIGN:
Andrew Bennett

WHILE SPEAKING at the St. Augustine Tiny House Festival (over 60,000 in attendance!), I had a chance to explore not only tiny houses but also campers, vintage RVs, house-bus conversions ("skoolies"), yurts, and vardos. And, yes, I snapped a ton of photos. Gypsy-wagon-like vardos are often overlooked in the tiny house scene. However, many of them manage to squeeze in a bathroom, heat, cooking and food prep space, and ample-enough storage, so there's good reason to have a look. Andrew Bennett's vardo has succeeded on all those counts.

"But Deek, this is just a tiny weekend camper — no one actually *lives* in structures this small. They couldn't!" Why not? Not only did Andrew Bennett and his crew at Trekker Trailers manage to work in a bathroom and shower space in a mere 50 square feet, but this little home on wheels has a TV, seating (not counting the bed), and a clever little slide-out desk that comes from under the sleeping platform to meet those sitting on the padded bench. There is even a small refrigerator in this li'l guy. And it just so happens that this structure *is* lived in full-time by a park ranger.

While the park ranger does have occasional guests (the bench can elongate into another bed space!), let's be honest: it would be too tight to have more than one person in 50 square feet for very long. Extremely small spaces also work better in some climates than others (in colder climates you might get a serious case of cabin fever). So 50 square feet isn't for everyone — heck, it's barely for anyone — but it is doable.

For storage, the space under the bed can be accessed from outside in the rear of trailer. This saves space by eliminating the need for a large, swinging interior door.

The tiny bathroom is a "wet-bath" — a toilet and shower stall in one.

IN RETROSPECT:

"I wish I'd done these sooner. The design is near perfection. I'm the first to admit my own shortcomings, too. I'll also add that you should be careful with your choices on heating and cooling. Research your systems and don't be dazzled and lured in by the lowest price — it may come back to haunt you."

For cooking, Andrew stows a hotplate in the cabinet.

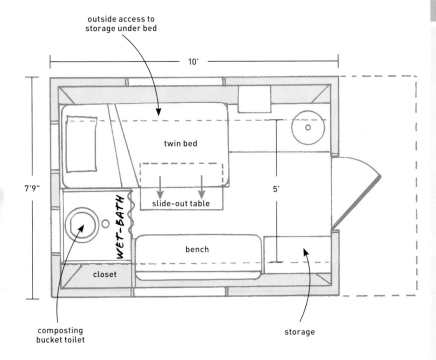

outside access to storage under bed

10'

7'9"

twin bed

slide-out table

5'

WET-BATH

bench

closet

composting bucket toilet

storage

I must say that while this is one of the tinier tinies you'll see, I found it to be one of the better thought-out and appealing homes I've seen in a while. "Bow tops," with their curved framing, create a gentle transition from wall to ceiling, blurring the boundary where the wall ends and the ceiling begins, which makes a small space feel a bit larger. However, they are difficult to construct and therefore difficult to fix and renovate.

While there isn't much going on with decor in this little trailer, there really isn't a need or the space for it. Andrew has incorporated a beautiful stained glass piece in the door, though. When you think you have no space for aesthetic touches, consider how you can make the functional aspects of your home artistic.

ANDREW'S VARDO STATS

DIMENSIONS: 10' long × 7'9" wide × 6'6" tall

SQUARE FOOTAGE: 65 (50 on the floor, but the walls step out)

BUDGET: $15,900 (retail price)

HEATING/COOLING: 5,000 Btu wall unit and space heater

BATHROOM: Wet bath with composting bucket toilet

HOT WATER: Ecotemp L5 Portable Tankless Water Heater (Andrew: "I don't recommend it.")

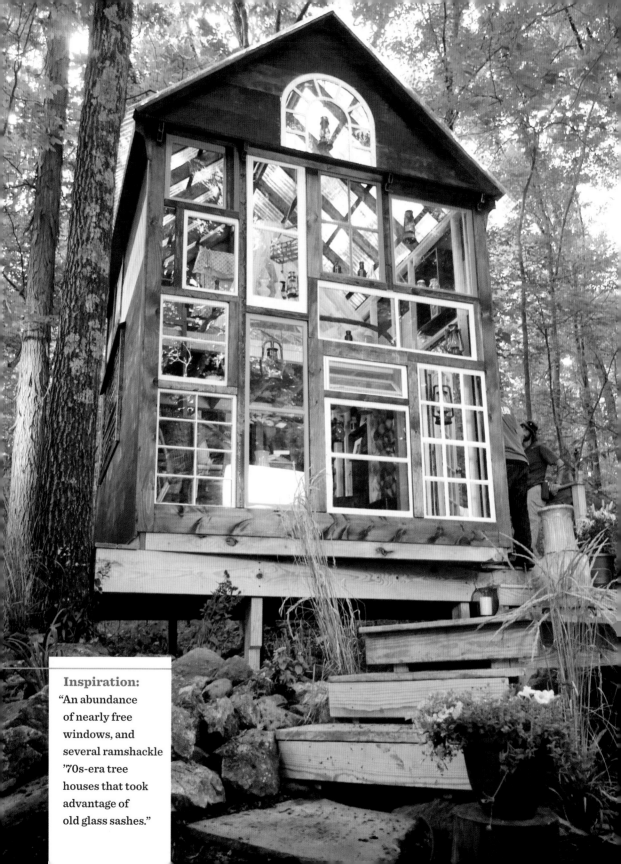

Inspiration:
"An abundance of nearly free windows, and several ramshackle '70s-era tree houses that took advantage of old glass sashes."

The Wall of Windows Tree House

LUNENBURG, MASSACHUSETTS

DESIGN:
Derek "Deek" Diedricksen

THE **"W.O.W." TREE HOUSE** is something I designed while hosting, building, and designing for our show *Tiny House Builders* on TV. Admittedly, it's not exactly a tiny house by most definitions, but I wanted to include it so I could point out what worked here and what didn't.

First, you arrive by crossing a wooden bridge over a small stream and then ascending two mini deck levels. At nearly 20 feet in the air, one side of this house sits on concrete posts, while the other side is bolted to two shagbark hickory trees. Once inside, you'll find yourself looking down through 2-inch-thick sheets of clear Lexan to the stream below (I'll warn you that Lexan is expensive). A wall of windows opens your view out to the forest. Cobbled together with windows from a salvage store, the wall cost only around $250, including the framing wood. The whole structure was framed with 2×6s to create wide window ledges for decorative glass items.

This getaway was meant for seasonal use, and our budget was limited. Therefore, it is not insulated, but it could be with a small investment of time and money, and the roof could be constructed with true decking, roofing paper, and standing seams. This place does have heat, however, by means of an electric fireplace, as well as a wine fridge, hammocks for lounging, a loft you can stand in with a queen-size bed, a television, and even a small kitchenette.

I love the wall of windows — it's the centerpiece of the whole tree house — but keep in mind that a wall like this, if it weren't in the deep shade of a forest, would cause you to roast in most climates, even with good ventilation. In our case, in the New England winters when the leaves are down, we really do want that solar gain, so this approach worked well for us. I would have provided natural light and ventilation for the bathroom, but we just didn't have time on a four-and-a-half-day "build 'n' shoot." Yes, there is a bathroom: hidden behind a very large salvage-constructed art piece that doubles as a swinging door is a 4 × 4-foot space with a composting toilet. We imagine this space could eventually be tiled and made into a wet-bath (shower and toilet stall in one).

"Secret" door to the bathroom

A window in the floor looks down to the stream below.

Lantern chandelier made from a vintage milk carrier

IN RETROSPECT: "I wish I'd had more time to build this. For example, we had about 10 minutes to put the vintage milk-carrier candle chandelier together before the camera crews kicked us out. While it works, it doesn't raise and lower on its pulleys as smoothly as it could. Also, the bathroom has a dark, 'crypt of doom' feel because we ran out of clear roofing and were way out in the woods."

THE WALL OF WINDOWS TREE HOUSE STATS

DIMENSIONS: 12' long × 10' wide × 20' tall

SQUARE FOOTAGE: Main area: 136; loft: 60

BUDGET: $6,000

HEATING/COOLING: Electric fireplace for heat (runs off a propane generator)

BATHROOM: Envirolet composting toilet

POWER: 5,000-watt generator

HOT WATER: Carried in and heated on a propane stove

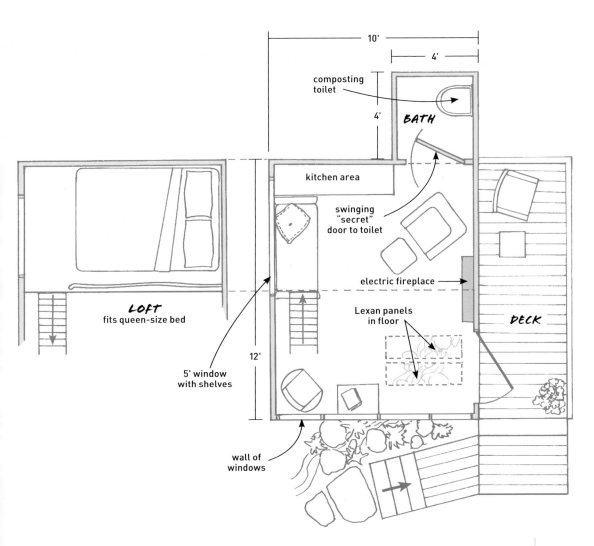

The Silver Bullet Tiny House

NEWBURYPORT,
MASSACHUSETTS

DESIGN:
Vera Struck

VERA STRUCK, who attended one of our first hands-on building workshops, is living proof that anyone can build a tiny home if they're willing to gather up a little know-how and stay the course. Situated on dual axles and only 18 feet long, Vera's tiny house is mostly noteworthy for what's on the inside. Take, for example, her thrifty use of wine boxes as kitchen drawers, her storage-as-steps ("tansu" steps) partially assembled from reused furniture, and her road-worthy bookshelf — all borne of the mind-set to work with what is available.

Vera's home also stands out as a demonstration of off-grid, low-impact living. Its name comes from its quick, bullet-like aim toward a sustainable, net-zero lifestyle (and its corrugated metal cladding seems to support the moniker as well). Vera gets energy via the Silver Bullet's solar panels, and she collects rain off the roof and channels it to a high-end marine filtering system. In the winter, Tuftex-covered door panels on the porch create an airlock, a buffer zone that enables her to conserve heat and reduce drafts, as well as keep snow and rain out of her home each time she opens the door. It's a tiny house that could appeal to both the vacation-getaway crowd and the "prepper" set.

Inspiration: "The work of Dee Williams, Jay Shafer, and Deek Diedricksen."

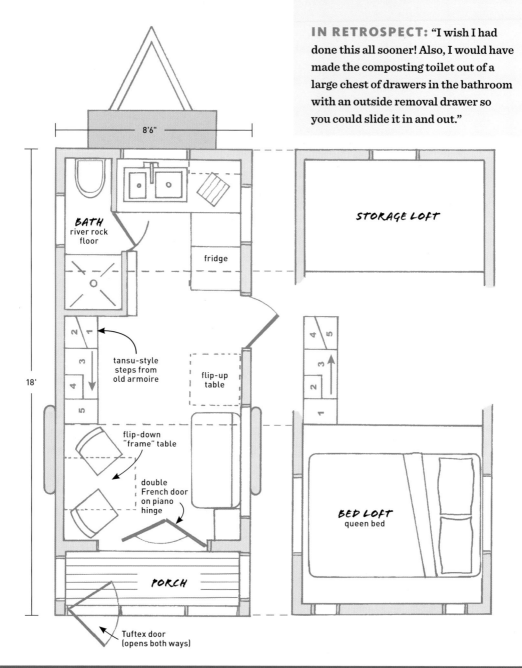

IN RETROSPECT: "I wish I had done this all sooner! Also, I would have made the composting toilet out of a large chest of drawers in the bathroom with an outside removal drawer so you could slide it in and out."

8'6"

STORAGE LOFT

BATH
river rock floor

fridge

18'

tansu-style steps from old armoire

flip-up table

flip-down "frame" table

double French door on piano hinge

BED LOFT
queen bed

PORCH

Tuftex door (opens both ways)

THE SILVER BULLET TINY HOUSE STATS

DIMENSIONS: 18' long × 8'6" wide × 13'4" tall

SQUARE FOOTAGE: Main area: 135; lofts (two): 105

BUDGET: $19,850

HEATING/COOLING: 750-watt ceramic electric heater (the house is super-insulated)

BATHROOM: Composting toilet with a urine diverter; shower

POWER: Renogy solar system

HOT WATER: 4-gallon electric water heater

Magnetic spice rack

DEEK'S TAKEAWAYS

Vera's porch stands out to me as well worth the space it takes up. It offers some outdoor living space and gives the home an appealing entrance. Granted, she could have instead built a detached mini deck, which would have allowed for more interior space, but Vera's choice is the more aesthetically pleasing one, and she now has a place for plants, outdoor seating, and meditating.

In addition, the large dormers increase Vera's side-to-side sleep space in what would otherwise be an incredibly cramped loft, and they add light and ventilation through their windows. Other highlights include the magnetic spice racks in the kitchen, the inclusion of both a back and side door (most tiny homes have only one), and the rather large bay window, which opens up the place and makes it feel far less walled in.

The "Reuse" Box Truck

HINGHAM, MASSACHUSETTS

DESIGN:
Derek "Deek" Diedricksen
and Alex Eaves

Inspiration:
"The need for Alex to live inexpensively, and to meld our skill sets into an educational project and film."

I AM ONE OF THE TWO PEOPLE responsible for the "Reuse" Box Truck. I was the lead builder and co-designer for this mobile dwelling and educational vehicle. What exactly does that mean? Well, filmmaker Alex Eaves ("dude two" of the team-up) was looking for a tour vehicle for his screenings and talks for the film *Reuse: Because You Can't Recycle the Planet*, and he suggested outfitting a retired moving truck as his home. It was also to be used as a merchandise booth, screening room, and real-life example of what reclamation and reuse could do. On my urging, what originally was going to be a 10-minute film on building, designing, and retrofitting a decommissioned 17-foot U-Haul quickly morphed into plans for a feature-length documentary. Once the project was crowd-funded, I brought in piles of my own salvage and roadside finds, alongside other secondhand items. Construction was soon underway, in the summer of 2016.

What we came up with on our meager budget, and while trying to use almost all salvaged and found materials, was a bare-bones dwelling that incorporated materials ranging from old bed parts, planks from a neighbor's dismantled fence, and dresser drawer sections to castaway 2×4s, plywood, pallet wood, and, well, just about everything but the kitchen sink. Wait . . . actually, we had one of those, too! Our plumbed-in sink is made from an old metal lobster pot.

One noteworthy aspect of this space is the abundance of natural light — something often lacking in container spaces. The large window by the entrance is actually a discarded sliding door (half of a set). When this house is on the move, the window will eventually have a Tuftex shutter for protection. Also to improve travel safety, we framed the window in place with stops, sealed it with an abundance of silicone, and cushioned it by first shimming it in place and then filling the flex spaces around the perimeter with Great Stuff foam insulation. After the foam dried, we removed the shims, so the window is supported directly by the foam and not the wood frame and held in place with trim. Thanks to this window, you're not looking into a wood or metal wall as you sit down at the makeshift desk, lounge on the day bed (made from a single, huge 12-foot pallet), or recline in the upper bed. Because moisture and mold can be problematic in container structures, we also made sure to include a few windows to keep the space ventilated.

We lucked out with many salvaged finds in this project. The overall message: By simply taking the time to plan ahead, scour through materials, and save what might be usable, you may be able to save boatloads of money and time (even if that boat is toy-size). On the other hand, I should warn you that it is possible to have *too* much time to collect materials. Then you'll be faced with keeping all your great "junk" safe, dry, and in some semblance of order. This can be more time- and energy-consuming than one might think. Believe me.

We found the armoire (a vintage canning cupboard) on the roadside and repaired and repainted it a little (retaining its funky patina) and were thus saved from having to build much storage space.

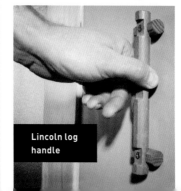

Lincoln log handle

A door handle made from skateboard trucks

The offset bunks aren't ideal for a couple, but they worked with the shape of the truck.

The calico wall of salvage wood adds character.

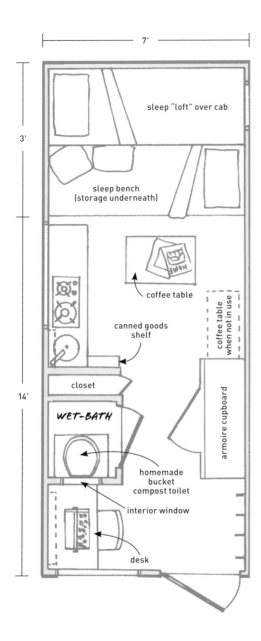

7'

3'

sleep "loft" over cab

sleep bench
(storage underneath)

coffee table

coffee table when not in use

canned goods shelf

closet

14'

WET-BATH

armoire cupboard

homemade
bucket
compost toilet

interior window

desk

THE "REUSE" BOX TRUCK STATS

DIMENSIONS: 14' long × 7' wide × 7' tall (with almost another 3' of space in the little lofted bunk)

SQUARE FOOTAGE: 98

BUDGET: Under $10,000 (including the truck for $8,000)

HEATING/COOLING: Electric space heater

BATHROOM: Wet bath with homemade bucket-style composting toilet

POWER: RV cord hookup with some supplemental solar lighting from Voltaic Systems mini solar panels

HOT WATER: Heated by range (for cooking and washing in the wet-bath)

Come shower time, just pick up this light toilet by the handles and move it so it doesn't get soaked.

IN RETROSPECT: "Having to film it all while building this was a pain. It slowed us down many times and killed our momentum. I also wish we could have had more windows, but our wall space for built-ins and storage was so limited that two were all we could fit."

The Turtleback

ANYWHERE, MONTANA

DESIGN:
Dave Emmons
and Zane Spang

ZANE SPANG IS A NOMAD, plain and simple. And while this Native American officially calls the mountains of Montana home, half his year is spent on the road, whether he's with his girlfriend and son or traveling alone. He is a man who lives by the seat of his pants and loves road trips and the prospect of adventure — and that's exactly how we met. Zane asked if he could come out and visit during the tiny house and tree house building workshop I was hosting on the off-grid property of Steven Harrell (see Steven's Cheer Stand, page 171). Little did we know that his "visit" entailed a solo drive from Montana to North Carolina! We're glad he made the trek, though, as his little home on wheels is simple living at its smallest and most basic, without sacrificing good design and good looks.

Take, for example, the "turtle shell" arched roof that Zane candidly admitted was "quite the challenge and learning experience, from force-bending wood with ratchet straps to making sure the roof channeled water correctly." He could have built a regular gable or shed-style roof, but that little bit of fancifulness was a must for Zane.

Inspiration: "We first looked at designing a teardrop trailer but eventually decided on adding more standing space. Our goal was to have a tiny-home feel in a camper-style structure."

I had the chance to camp out and chat with Zane over our three-day workshop in the woods. This was plenty of time to get an honest take on what it's really like to travel, live, or stay in something so, well, "micro." Zane, time and time again, professed how he loved it and how freeing it was, especially the ability to pull over just about anywhere for a good night's sleep. He also was honest enough to admit his wagon's spatial shortcomings. "I've found out that it's very doable — even great — for one person, but when we've traveled with our baby, it just gets tight really fast."

Zane's wagon might not be considered a true tiny house by some standards, but it features most, if not all, of the requirements for living, including storage, cooking space, ventilation, a full-size bed, and even a stowed composting toilet. Okay, going to the bathroom in a tiny open space inches away from where you sleep is not a dream scenario for most, but you could instead take the toilet outdoors or into a curtained space, for example. Zane does not live in this tiny travel trailer on wheels full-time, but if push came to shove, I have no doubt that he could, even if it meant rigging a camp-style solar shower outside the dwelling. In any case, Zane's wagon offers many ideas, and it might prompt you to ask, "Just how tiny could I go?"

Zane's camper from its skeletal beginnings to road-ready completion.

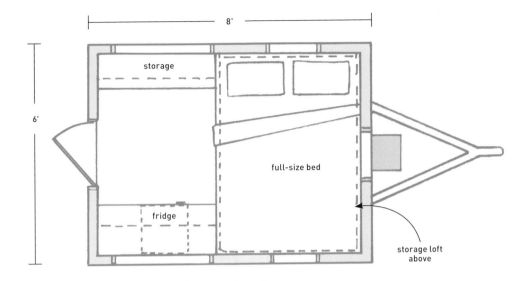

storage

8'

6'

full-size bed

fridge

storage loft
above

IN RETROSPECT: "I probably would not build it with so much tongue weight, as the trailer had a couple issues in the front. Also, we used a refrigerator to keep food cool, but a high-performance cooler of some sort would have done just as well. Other than that, it sleeps very cozy and is a great travel tiny home for extended trips. I could live in this home during the summer in the Rocky Mountains. It has freed up finances and allows me to take my own space with me wherever I wish to go."

DIMENSIONS: 8' long × 6' wide × 8' tall

SQUARE FOOTAGE: 48

BUDGET: $2,000

HEATING/COOLING: Air conditioner and a portable heater; also a Breeze window fan to circulate air throughout the home.

BATHROOM: Composting toilet space when needed for longer trips

POWER: Two rechargeable 6-volt marine batteries connected to 12-volt/120-watt outlets

HOT WATER: Portable solar shower bag rigged with a hula-hoop shower curtain, or water heated by a gas burner

The XS

DESIGN:
**Tumbleweed
Tiny House Company**

Y ET ANOTHER TUMBLEWEED tiny house design might lead you to think that I work for them, or that honcho Steve Weissman is a cousin or former college mate, but no, I do not, and he was not. The Tumbleweed Tiny House Company has been around for a long, long time, and their staying power is rooted in good design, clean and appealing lines, and innovation. I find the XS model you're seeing here particularly attractive in almost a novelty dollhouse way. Great on many levels, it also has elements that need improvement. Designs and products evolve over time, which is one reason why this house was taken off the company's roster long ago. And its diminutive size just wasn't popular among consumers. These days, tiny homes are getting larger and larger, as are the demands on trailer axles.

I'll start by saying that, yes, you can live in this house full-time. Don't take my word for it, though — ask Chris Haynes, now a tiny house designer, who lived in these 66 square feet for almost two years while saving money to buy land and build the comparatively massive 292-square-foot home he now resides in (a plan-altered Tumbleweed Bodega). While the bath-room situation in this structure (a mere 2 × 4-foot wet-bath stall with a composting toilet) might be a deal-breaker for some, at least there *is* a bathroom. And it's all designed to sit atop a single axle, though this particular version was built on skids.

When not in use, the tiny ladder hangs against the side wall so as not to block what little counter space there is.

What's most surprising to those who step into this ultra-tiny is that it actually has a loft! Through the little hobbit-like crawl hole there is a full house-length loft with a tiny window for light, ventilation, and possible emergency exit, though Chris admits that he slept on the mini couch below. Still, there is something kind of neat about so tiny a sleep space, in a kid's-fort kind of way — unless you're prone to claustrophobia!

DEEK'S TAKEAWAYS

I happen to own the particular little house you see here, so I'm well acquainted with it and can tell you both the good and the bad. I love that Tumbleweed was able to fit so much into so small a space — it's a work of mathematical art. This little space is also bright, which helps it feel less cell-like, but the loft is just too hard to get to, and, furthermore, requires that you step on your food-prep counter to squeeze your way up. However, it's the lack of an open cathedral ceiling that really makes this space, and the loft, feel smaller than it could. Even a more open loft entrance by the front door would have helped. There's a lesson in visual space to be learned here, and it's one of the reasons that Tumbleweed abandoned their crawl-hole lofts a long time ago. Smart move.

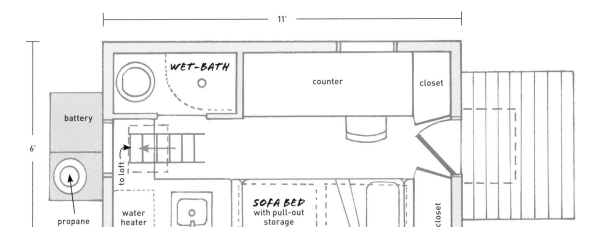

Plan dimensions: 11' (width) × 6' (depth)

Labels within floor plan:
- WET-BATH
- counter
- closet
- battery
- to loft
- propane tank
- water heater
- SOFA BED with pull-out storage
- closet

THE XS STATS

DIMENSIONS: 11' long × 6' wide × 10' tall

SQUARE FOOTAGE: Main area: 66; loft: 40

BUDGET: Approximately $6,000

HEATING/COOLING: Electric space heater (woodstove originally)

BATHROOM: Wet bath with homemade composting toilet (a bucket with sawdust and peat moss)

POWER: Electric tapped off adjacent house, with former solar DC hookups/outlets remaining

HOT WATER: Tankless propane water heater

IN RETROSPECT: "The loft access was just too small, never mind the loft itself, so I mainly used it for storage. I also would have added extra insulation to the floor — something people often cheap out on — as on some really cold nights, the dog's dish would freeze to the floor."

Shelving underneath stairs

The Carl Ultralight

CLEVELAND, OHIO

DESIGN:
Carl Baldesare,
Small Spaces CLE

Inspiration:
"Tiny house daydreams and the challenge of building a lighter, easier-to-haul tiny house."

CARL BALDESARE sums up this dual-axle tiny home rather succinctly when he says, "Really, it's meant as a bachelor or bachelorette pad and little more." But it's still one of the nicer, simpler, and smaller tiny houses I've seen. The team at Small Spaces CLE (led by Packy Hyland) took a few steps toward "tiny luxury" without overdoing it at all. While many people might be more attracted to the high-end homes that have every bell, whistle, and doohickey imaginable, there is also a large league of tiny fans who prefer to keep things affordable and nearly bare-bones. This model, however, would prevent most people from feeling they're "roughing it" in any sense.

The Carl Ultralight has a spacious bathroom, beautiful live-edge countertops, a custom built-in writing nook, and stairs-as-shelves. Add to that a convection oven for baking and an induction cooktop that heats up a pot but not so much the air around it — a great choice for most tiny homes. Carl and his crew have effectively hidden much more within a 16-foot travel trailer than you might suspect. Plus, this build is so small and light (steel-framed with spray foam insulation) that it can be easily towed, maneuvered, and even hidden.

I'm a big fan of the rectangular awning windows and the custom-built L-shaped couch (with storage beneath it, of course!). But it's the light and calming whitewashed walls that really give this one an edge. Pickling finishes such as this are easy to apply, and they "give the interior some nice color, all without too heavy an application," as Carl puts it. They also allow the grain of the wood to show through the stain.

What I had never seen until my visit, however, was the use of a ½-inch tempered glass safety railing for the loft — pure genius. Many homes have bulky and often clumsy loft railings, but this short glass wall opens up the space so much more. The CLE team also designed high knee walls on the sides of the loft, along with a shallow-pitch gable roof, for more usable space and headroom. As for what I'd change, I'd put in a larger sink and add a skylight in the loft, or at least a larger window for emergency egress and a nap view.

Live-edge countertop and induction stovetop

Kick drawer under the oven

IN RETROSPECT:
"I think our biggest mistake was not making the stairs wide enough. Also, a longer stair run would have been better. Newer models now have much better stairs. You live and learn. I would also do an 18-foot trailer next time for our smallest build (assuming stairs instead of a ladder)."

The loft includes a tempered glass safety wall.

DIMENSIONS: 16' long (plus trailer tongue) × 8'6" wide × 13'5" tall

SQUARE FOOTAGE: Main area: 128; loft: 60

BUDGET: $68,000

HEATING/COOLING: 9,000 Btu Mitsubishi mini split (with "Hyper-Heating," designed for cold climates)

BATHROOM: Flush toilet to septic, sewer, or RV holding tank; shower

POWER: 50-amp RV cord hookup

HOT WATER: 2-gallon, 120-volt electric water heater

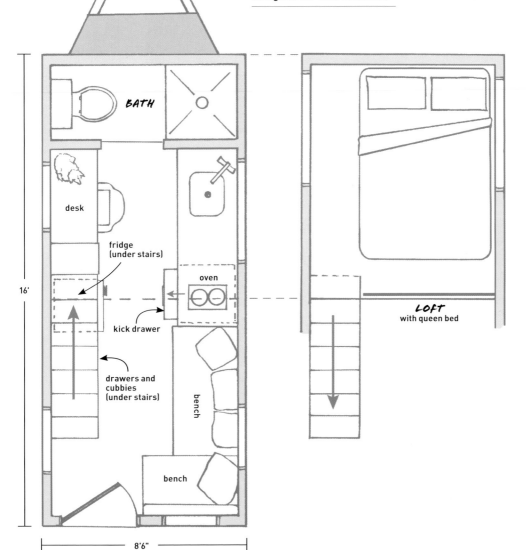

16'

8'6"

BATH

desk

fridge (under stairs)

oven

kick drawer

drawers and cubbies (under stairs)

bench

bench

LOFT with queen bed

The Kenney Camper

(1966 DuPage Cloud Coach)

**ANYWHERE
THEY WANT TO BE**

DESIGN:
DuPage Coach of
Wood Dale, Illinois
(original camper);
Steve and Emily Kenney
(redesign)

Inspiration:
"Getting away from
it all. Freedom."

TAKE A 12-FOOT DUPAGE CAMPER from the 1960s, gut it, restyle it as your own, and travel the "tin can tourist" circuit? Yes, please. And that is exactly what Steve and Emily Kenney did. There are a great many full-time camper dwellers in the United States and beyond, and this mode of living has a lot in common with the tiny house scene. The worlds of campers, boats, tree houses, gypsy wagons, cabins, and yurts are all cut from the same cloth and rely on a wealth of ingenuity when it comes to spatial efficiency.

In the particular case of the Kenney Camper, we're dealing with not only a great layout but also a ton of personal charm and style. Each piece of this 12-footer, and every aspect of decor and storage, has been carefully crafted and selected. Take, for example, the storage over the counter. While most campers have boxy cabinets to hide everything away, the Kenneys chose custom backlit shelving that actually serves as both a decorative element and a source of light. Lighting, both natural and installed, is key with these tiny campers. As with many structures in this book, the very open floor plan is also a big part of what makes it all work so well.

Sink cover

Wet-bath

The seating bay transforms to a sleeper for two — nothing new in the camper or tiny house world, but that's because it works.

DEEK'S TAKEAWAYS

The wet-bath is one of the smallest I've seen, perhaps with the exception of the Trekker Trailers vardo (page 189), but it still gets the job done. Remember, we're dealing with a 7 × 12-foot structure here. To eat up any more living space in exchange for a booth that's used for a mere 20 to 30 minutes a day wouldn't make that much sense.

The sink cover adds a little more counter space when the sink is not in use. It's not much, but I appreciate the attention to detail. And remember, all the tiny bits of space saved, or dual-purposed, add up.

Backlit shelving

IN RETROSPECT: "A hanging closet would have been nice — it's something often overlooked in small space designs and more useful and important than most realize."

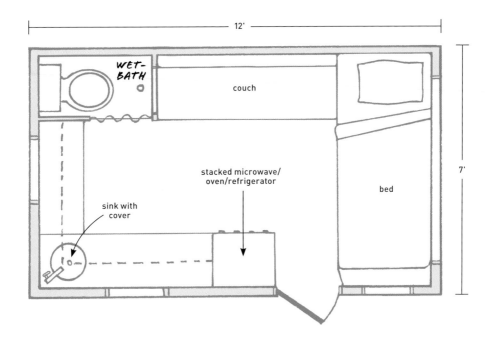

WET-BATH

couch

bed

stacked microwave/
oven/refrigerator

sink with
cover

12'

7'

THE KENNEY CAMPER STATS

DIMENSIONS: 12' long × 7' wide × 6'3" tall;
15' long with trailer tongue

SQUARE FOOTAGE: 84

BUDGET: $6,000

HEATING/COOLING: 9,500 Btu Coleman
Mach3 Cub with heat strip

BATHROOM: Wet bath with flush toilet to
RV septic hookup or tank

POWER: 30-amp RV cord hookup

HOT WATER: 8-gallon tank-style electric
water heater

Funky East Austin Tiny House

MOST OF LIFE'S NECESSITIES scrunched into just 12 feet? Yep. Here's another one that sounds implausible, but thanks to Greg Parham and crew at Rocky Mountain Tiny Houses, it's a reality. In fact, it's their most famous tiny house to date. Featuring a kitchen situated up front, living space in the middle, a bathroom in the rear, and one of the cooler yet simpler lofts I've seen (it actually hangs from the ceiling at one corner), this house was created for the backyard rental scene. Part of its wide appeal is its unique style combination of rustic and steampunk. A multitude of pipe fittings tie together the towel racks, light fixtures, toilet paper holder, shelving, and pot racks, offsetting the country vibe.

Add to this some funky glass lamp hoods, an array of modern windows without divided panes, and a very attractive barn-wood door, and it's no surprise that this has been a flagship home for Rocky Mountain Tiny Houses.

AUSTIN, TEXAS

DESIGN:
Greg Parham
and Rocky Mountain
Tiny Houses

Inspiration:
"Rocky Mountain
Tiny Houses'
16-foot Boulder
model."

The lighting and the hanging seating (almost like a porch swing indoors) are among the most successful focus points in this build, but it's the welded square-channel loft frame that I really dig. Here's why: Building with steel (far stronger than wood) allows the supporting members of the loft to be constructed with 1½- or 2-inch-deep stock instead of their 3½- or 5½-inch lumber counterparts, saving several inches of height. Again, in spaces so incredibly tiny, every inch counts, especially with headroom. I also love the simple, tough-as-nails corrugated exterior siding. It fits the client's needs, it's affordable, it goes up quickly, and it will last a long, long time.

Pipe fittings add a steampunk element.

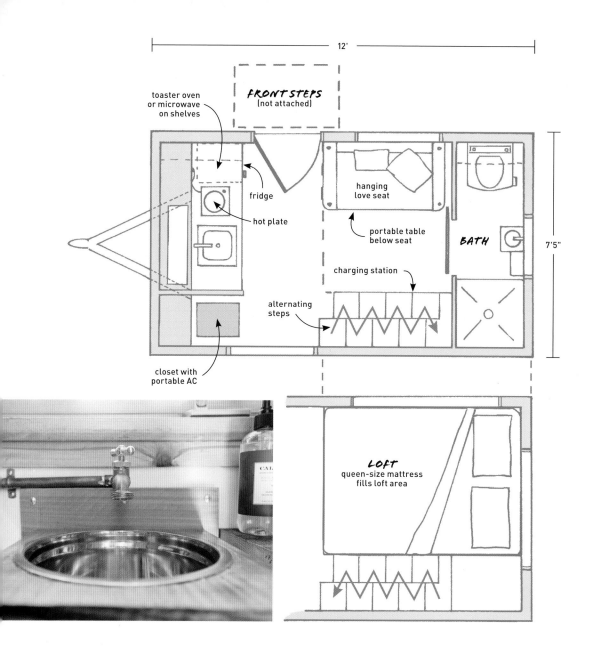

12'

FRONT STEPS
(not attached)

toaster oven
or microwave
on shelves

fridge

hot plate

hanging
love seat

portable table
below seat

BATH

7'5"

charging station

alternating
steps

closet with
portable AC

LOFT
queen-size mattress
fills loft area

FUNKY EAST AUSTIN TINY HOUSE STATS

DIMENSIONS: 12' long × 7'5" wide × 13'3" tall

SQUARE FOOTAGE: Main area: 88; loft: 50

BUDGET: $27,000

HEATING/COOLING: Envi electric wall-mount heater; portable window-mount air conditioner

BATHROOM: Incinolet incinerating toilet; shower

POWER: Grid-tied

HOT WATER: Tankless electric water heater for the bathroom; small electric point-of-use tank in kitchen

The live-edge maple stairs give a natural touch to an otherwise industrial look.

IN RETROSPECT: "From a design standpoint, the prow on the front wall is cool, but it complicated the build and made it difficult to use the gained space, since the wall angles out. But all in all it is a neat feature, and I don't necessarily regret it. I just mention it more to warn people of its complications."

The CAFAM Cabin

LOS ANGELES, CALIFORNIA

DESIGN:
Derek "Deek" Diedricksen

Inspiration:
"Shipping container homes and budget constraints."

THIS SHELL OF A CABIN, not yet outfitted as a tiny house, was built at a workshop at the Craft and Folk Art Museum in Los Angeles in 2017. The exterior was painted by native LA artist Charlie Edmiston. I'm showing it here as an example of an incredibly simple, open, and exposed build in the hope that it might help some aspiring designers who are gunning for a budget-minded small structure. The goal of our project was to see what a group of complete novices (in most cases) could do in a mere 30 hours over 2 days.

This little guy is just 7 × 15 feet and thus geared toward use as a backyard workshop, studio, office, or guest space — maybe even a weekend getaway cabin — but a space like this does have tiny house potential, easily. Many of the early tiny houses on wheels from the late '90s were 16 feet or even smaller. Knowing this, you might start to see that with the incorporation of some storage, a tiny 3 × 3-foot wet-bath (which there's space for), a kitchenette across from the front door, and a little Envi heater or Dickinson marine heater, you'd be well on your way to a very affordable, downscaled living situation. A structure like this could also be used for temporary disaster relief.

See the detailed framing plans beginning on page 242.

There is a bit more to this structure than might meet the eye. First, the design aims to use materials as close as possible to their purchase lengths, for the sake of economy. For example, while the 7 × 15-foot floor seems odd, it allowed us to use standard plywood sheets for the 8 × 16-foot roof and have a 6-inch overhang on all sides. The scraps left over from building the floor and the 7-feet-and-change walls were later reworked into the front "art window."

The porch area, while not a usable space to plop any sort of deck chair or grill, breaks up the boxiness of the facade. By pushing this wall back a mere 2 feet, very little space was wasted, and the trade-off provides a place for potted plants and a dry overhang for when you're fumbling for your keys in the rain. This overhang also keeps the rain away from the front door.

There isn't a ton more to point out, other than what some might call a "bunk loft." Underneath this you could position another bed, dressers, beanbag seats, or storage. Note that we did not connect it to the front wall in order to allow an insulating curtain to be slid all the way across the 8-foot-wide Tuftex polycarbonate window. This helps keep the cabin warm or cool (as needed) and is a must for any sort of privacy. Glass windows could easily be substituted for the polycarbonate.

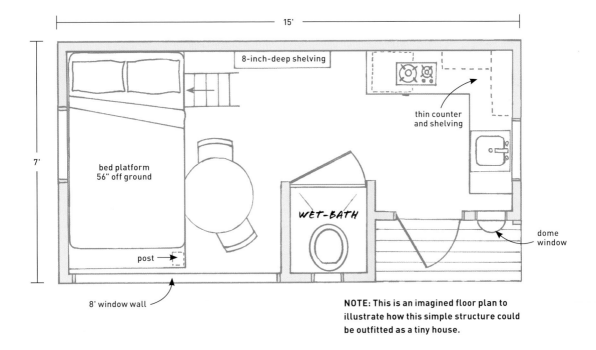

15'

7'

8-inch-deep shelving

thin counter
and shelving

bed platform
56" off ground

WET-BATH

post →

dome
window

8' window wall

NOTE: This is an imagined floor plan to illustrate how this simple structure could be outfitted as a tiny house.

THE CAFAM CABIN STATS

DIMENSIONS: 15' long × 7' wide × 8'6" tall

SQUARE FOOTAGE: 105

BUDGET: A little under $2,000

HEATING/COOLING: Electric Envi heater

BATHROOM: 3' × 3' space factored in for a wet-bath with composting toilet

POWER: External extension cord (for the time being), Voltaic Systems solar panel and LED lighting kit (which can also charge phones and laptops)

HOT WATER: None (to be added later, if desired)

IN RETROSPECT: "I wish we had time to build in a little kitchenette, but that would be for the future raffle winner to do, if desired. I also would have loved more protective overhangs, but we were trying to maximize use of stock materials while minimizing price. For more year-round use, I'd use glass for the front wall of windows — maybe even use two or three repurposed slider doors."

Before You Build

DEREK "DEEK" DIEDRICKSEN

SO, YOU'RE THINKING about setting out to build your own tiny home or structure. Congrats!

"But how do I get started?" People email me with this question all the time, and rightfully so. I mean, who wants to blindly jump into the alligator-infested pit of peril when it comes to building or designing a structure for the very first (or even fiftieth) time? There are so many things that can go wrong, not to mention how long it can take and how much it can cost.

Unfortunately, there is no short answer to this question, and because I'd like to stay in the good graces of my wife, spend some time with my kids, and do the things I need to do for a living, I can't always give a satisfactory response. So here's a cheat sheet, of sorts, to help you feel a bit more ready for the jump ahead (and you can find more tips spread throughout this book). After all, rushing into a project without thorough contemplation, daydreaming, and planning could be one of the more expensive mistakes you'll ever make.

**TAKE YOUR TIME.
DO IT RIGHT.
IT'S NOT A RACE.**

READY? HERE'S A BASIC RUNDOWN,
in no special order:

KNOW YOUR SITE. In addition to finding out if your build will be allowed on whatever piece of property you're dealing with, make sure you understand the natural and/or legal restrictions of your site. Are there any wetlands that you can't build near? Are there seasonal washes or floods in the area? Where will the arc of the sun pass in relation to where you'll position the build, and where do you want your windows to be (or not be) to take advantage of that? And so on . . .

DOWNSIZE, STARTING NOW. If you're transitioning to living in a tiny house full-time, you'll want to start whittling down your possessions (that is, unless you want to keep everything and spend a fortune on storage). Downsizing isn't an overnight endeavor. It's personal, painstaking, and tough, and it will take you three times as long as you think it will. Have a look at Ryan Nicodemus's essay about minimalism on page 162. The dude is a pro.

GATHER MATERIALS. If you plan on building with salvaged materials, start looking for and saving them now. You'll need lots of time and patience because you will not find your ingredients overnight — I promise you. I will also add a warning that planning and harvesting *too* much *too* early results in the cumbersome chores of storing, keeping track of, and maintaining your goods. The ol' pile with a tarp over it won't stay tarped for long. It will also look awful in your yard and possibly annoy close neighbors.

SPREAD THE WORD. Tell every soul who might care and who might be supportive of your endeavor. You'll be surprised at how many people are excited to help, lend tools, or donate materials for your future home.

RESEARCH, ABSORB. Go online, read books, check out plans, and soak up all the ideas and inspiration you can before you set about nailing the first board. Take your time. Proper planning will help you get what you want, and get it with less waste and fewer mistakes.

EXPERIENCE TINY. As part of your research, visit or spend a night in a tiny house rental (or as many as you can). There is no better way to get a sense of what might work and what might not than by actually being inside a tiny house (especially for people who aren't very visual). Renting a place for a night or two (through Airbnb, for example) allows you to take your sweet time and look around at every aspect of the house. How does the space flow? What would you change? Does it feature enough storage for your needs? Take photos, too — your memory may not be as good as you think it is.

IDENTIFY YOUR ESSENTIALS. Figure out what you really need by way of appliances and, well, everything else. For example, knowing what you need to plug in (and where)

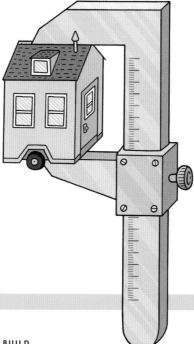

will save you time, money, hassle, and heartache when creating an electrical plan and determining where to add outlets. This will also prevent the old nightmare of running 8 feet of extension cord across the room to plug in your toaster, which is not only unsightly but also possibly dangerous.

LEARN ABOUT TRAILERS. If you're planning a wheeled build, acquire some basic knowledge on what to look for in a trailer. This is the very foundation of your home — the base that all of your time and money will rest upon. Make sure it's the right one. If you'd like to buy a used trailer (which I recommend less and less these days), bring along someone well versed in trailers or metalworking to look it over. Make sure it's safe and not going to cost you tenfold in the long run. There are a ton of blog articles, online discussion threads, and even sites on custom trailers for tiny houses — read as many of them as you can. This is the single most important purchase for your tiny house on wheels.

TAKE PHOTOS. Photograph everything you see that might inspire you or enhance your build. Pictures also can help you convey ideas to a builder, a hardware store employee, or a zoning board official, depending on the case. Plus, you'll be keeping visual notes on what you like. Dig a color scheme, a certain DIY railing, the way stairs were built, or the loft-less lay-out of a tiny house you happen to see? Take a photo. You're bound to forget the details if you don't.

CONSIDER A TINY HOUSE WORK-SHOP. There are seven zillion of them, but I recommend those where you actually get to use tools and build something (there are only a few, mine being one of them). There is no quicker way to learn, network, and be inspired than by doing it firsthand alongside many tiny house designers and build-ers. Workshops are a place to work out your kinks, too, instead of making costly mistakes on your own home, on your own dime. And they're a lot of fun! Do be sure to look for a host who has long-running experience in not only building, but building small — it's a very different ballgame in some respects.

TAPE IT OUT. Not sure what it would feel like to navigate an 8 × 24-foot house? Consider laying it out with masking tape in your driveway, a large hallway, or any other appropriate space you can find. You can then go a step further and tape out your interior walls, furniture, built-ins, and any-thing else you want to get a feel for.

PRACTICE BUILDING. You should have at least some background and basic experience with construction. If you don't own any tools, get a few of the essentials (carpentry hand tools, plus a circular saw and power drill-driver) and complete a small project or two before you dive headfirst into

building a house. Construction isn't rocket science, but it takes a steady hand, some skills, and patience, not to mention the right tools. Hop on a friend's home improvement project, offer to help with someone else's tiny house, or, heck, at least build a couple birdhouses and an Adirondack chair. Doing any of this will give you confidence and improve your chances of success with your much larger undertaking.

ASK FOR HELP. Tell yourself right now, "It's okay to ask for help." This is not the brag-a-thon some seem to make it out to be. You don't have to do every single thing yourself. It's perfectly all right, and often safer, to seek help. You won't be a failure or less of an "official" tiny house scenester for doing so.

PAD THE SCHEDULE. Plan on everything taking about three times as long as you think it will. It's just the way it is. Materials run out, tools get lost, weather gets bad, help doesn't show, you get sick . . . and it all adds up. This will take a long time. Don't fool yourself into thinking it won't.

All that being said, YOU CAN DO THIS. Those aren't just words. Some of my closest friends are absolute idiots, yet they churn out gorgeous handiwork time and again because they acknowledge the rules, the preparation needed, and the possible perils of building a tiny house.

All together now: "I Can Do This!"

The CAFAM Cabin Framing Plans

BONUS SECTION! Here is a set of framing plans that provide measurements, ideas, and multiple views for a basic build you might want to try out or use for inspiration. As the designer of the CAFAM Cabin, I wanted to offer up something darn affordable and accessible, a project that could be easily tackled by people of almost any skill level or background. So the framing plans that follow represent a really simple build — and therein might lie the beauty.

The CAFAM is named after the incredibly cool Craft and Folk Art Museum in Los Angeles, where we built the prototype structure (see page 233). The framing plans here are a hair bigger than the CAFAM model we actually built in Los Angeles. In a field where every inch counts, we figured we'd give this cabin a few more square feet while still using stock-length lumber where and when possible.

This blank slate of a cabin is just begging you to set up, tweak, divide, and use it per your own needs and tastes. After all, this book is about inspiration, with the hope that you'll grab all sorts of ideas from the various features and then implement them in your own perfect-for-you tiny structure. Likewise, these basic construction plans don't impose much of the designer's personal and specific tastes; rather, they invite you to deviate, daydream, add,

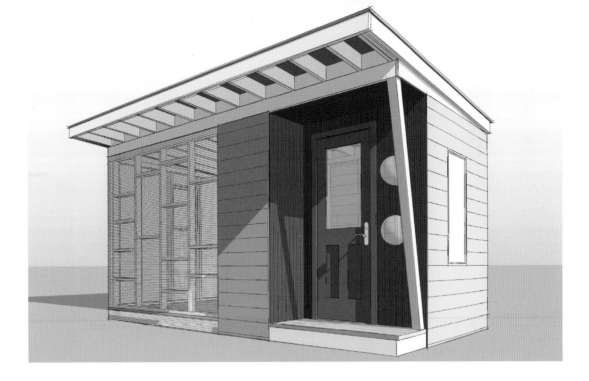

and subtract. That's why we kept it simple and versatile. Don't like the Tuftex front? Well, change it out with three repurposed double-pane sliders. The roof doesn't slope enough for your climate? You can increase the pitch with a simple alteration. Not crazy about the mini loft we showed you in the photo on page 234? Take it out.

Best of luck to you, and may this be at least a starting point for what could become a cool little greenhouse, backyard studio, workshop, or even — with a few simple adjustments and some insulation — a tiny house. Heck, I could even see this as a tree house. If you do tackle the CAFAM, I'd love to see it. Seek me out online and share some photos with me!

This blank slate of a cabin is just begging you to set up, tweak, divide, and use it per your own needs and tastes.

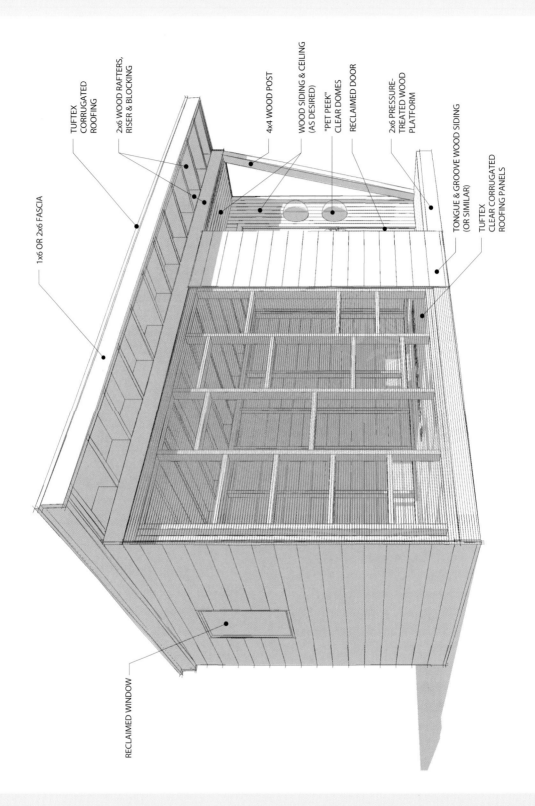

TUFTEX CORRUGATED ROOFING

2x6 WOOD RAFTERS, RISER & BLOCKING

4x4 WOOD POST

WOOD SIDING & CEILING (AS DESIRED)

"PET PEEK" CLEAR DOMES

RECLAIMED DOOR

2x6 PRESSURE-TREATED WOOD PLATFORM

TONGUE & GROOVE WOOD SIDING (OR SIMILAR)

TUFTEX CLEAR CORRUGATED ROOFING PANELS

1x6 OR 2x6 FASCIA

RECLAIMED WINDOW

EXPLODED VIEW

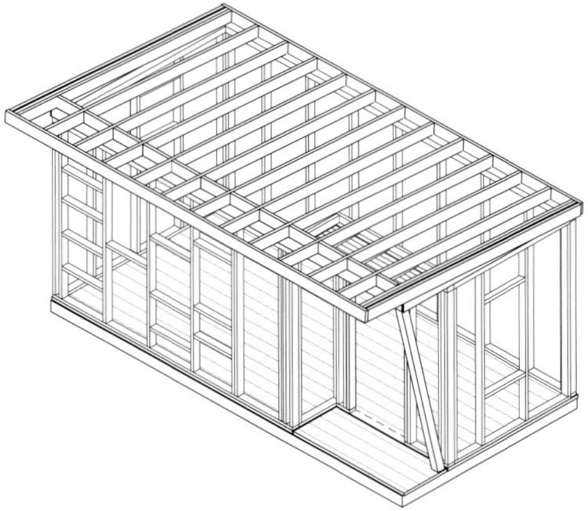

Fig. 1

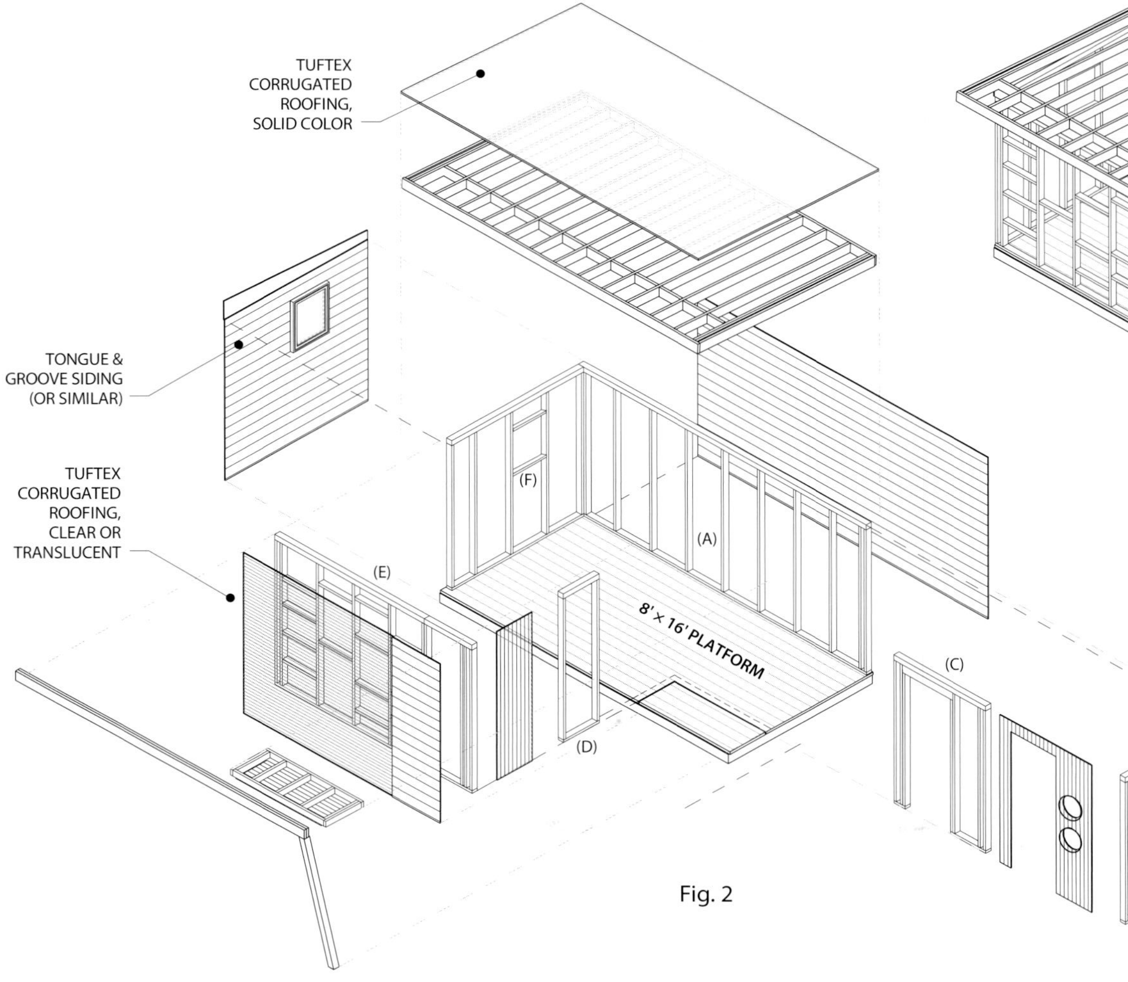

Fig. 2

8' × 16' PLATFORM

(A)
(B)
(C)
(D)
(E)
(F)

TUFTEX
CORRUGATED
ROOFING,
SOLID COLOR

TONGUE &
GROOVE SIDING
(OR SIMILAR)

TUFTEX
CORRUGATED
ROOFING,
CLEAR OR
TRANSLUCENT

245

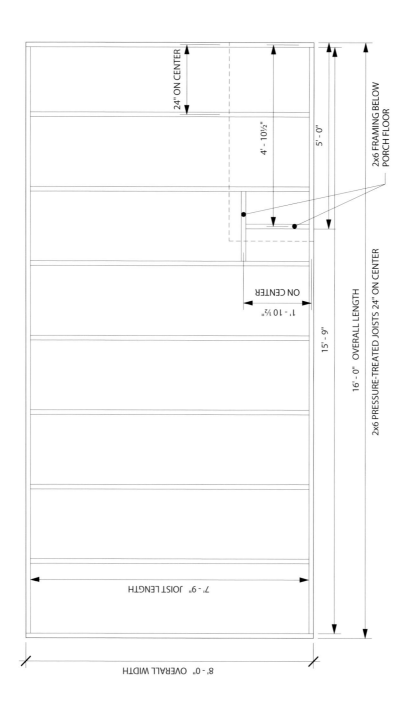

24" ON CENTER

4' - 10½"

5' - 0"

2x6 FRAMING BELOW PORCH FLOOR

1' - 10½"
ON CENTER

15' - 9"

16' - 0" OVERALL LENGTH

2x6 PRESSURE-TREATED JOISTS 24" ON CENTER

7' - 9" JOIST LENGTH

8' - 0" OVERALL WIDTH

PLAN/STUD LAYOUT

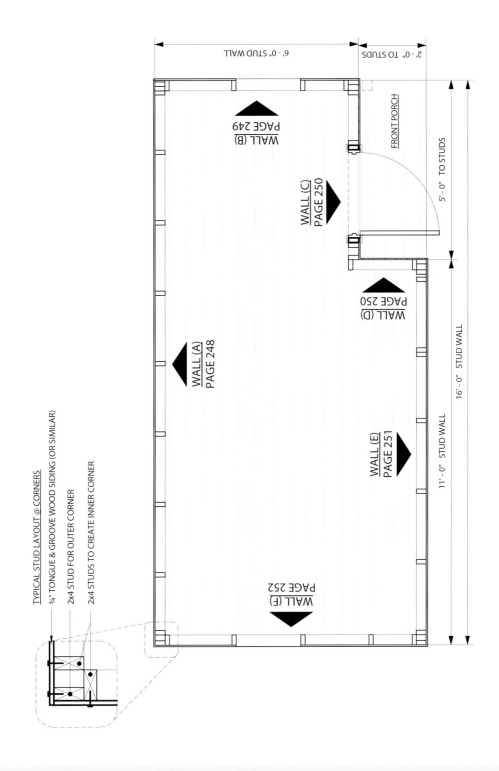

6' - 0" STUD WALL

2' - 0" TO STUDS

WALL (B)
PAGE 249

FRONT PORCH

5' - 0" TO STUDS

WALL (C)
PAGE 250

WALL (D)
PAGE 250

WALL (A)
PAGE 248

16' - 0" STUD WALL

WALL (E)
PAGE 251

11' - 0" STUD WALL

WALL (F)
PAGE 252

TYPICAL STUD LAYOUT @ CORNERS

¾" TONGUE & GROOVE WOOD SIDING (OR SIMILAR)

2x4 STUD FOR OUTER CORNER

2x4 STUDS TO CREATE INNER CORNER

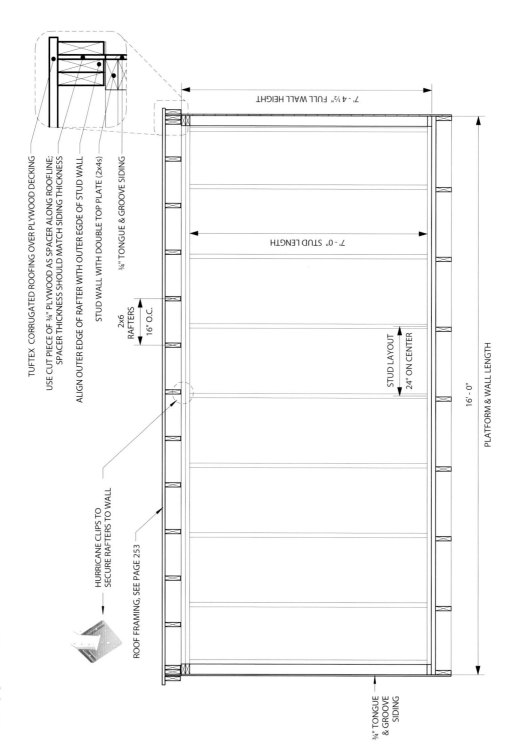

TUFTEX CORRUGATED ROOFING OVER PLYWOOD DECKING

USE CUT PIECE OF ¾" PLYWOOD AS SPACER ALONG ROOFLINE; SPACER THICKNESS SHOULD MATCH SIDING THICKNESS

ALIGN OUTER EDGE OF RAFTER WITH OUTER EDGE OF STUD WALL

STUD WALL WITH DOUBLE TOP PLATE (2x4s)

¾" TONGUE & GROOVE SIDING

2x6 RAFTERS
16" O.C.

HURRICANE CLIPS TO SECURE RAFTERS TO WALL

ROOF FRAMING, SEE PAGE 253

7'-4 ½" FULL WALL HEIGHT

7'-0" STUD LENGTH

STUD LAYOUT
24" ON CENTER

16'-0"
PLATFORM & WALL LENGTH

¾" TONGUE & GROOVE SIDING

WALL (B) FRAMING

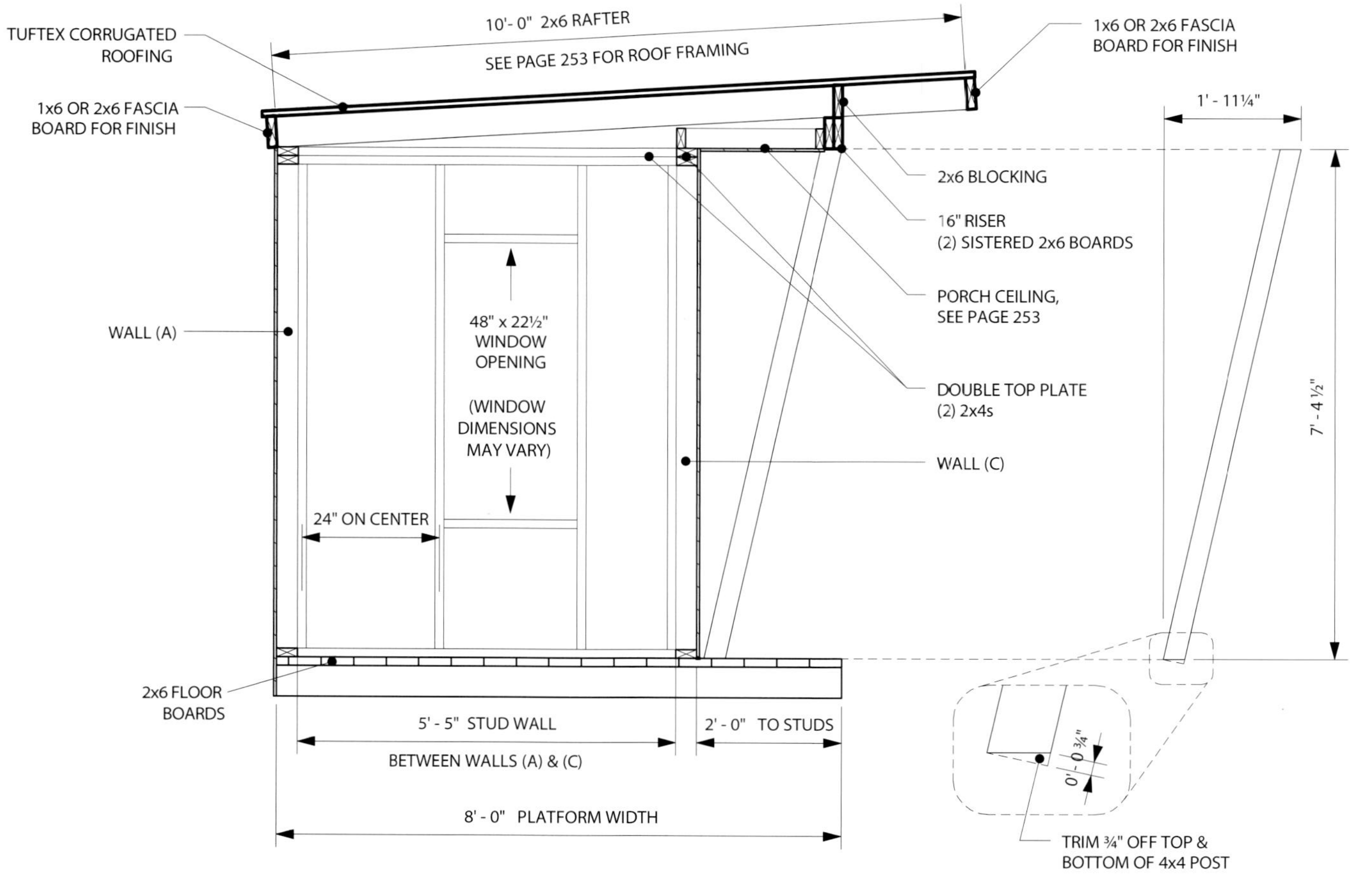

7' - 4½"

1' - 11¼"

1x6 OR 2x6 FASCIA
BOARD FOR FINISH

TRIM ¾" OFF TOP &
BOTTOM OF 4x4 POST

0' - 0 ⅜"

2x6 BLOCKING

16" RISER

(2) SISTERED 2x6 BOARDS

PORCH CEILING,
SEE PAGE 253

DOUBLE TOP PLATE
(2) 2x4s

WALL (C)

10' - 0" 2x6 RAFTER

SEE PAGE 253 FOR ROOF FRAMING

48" x 22½"
WINDOW
OPENING

(WINDOW
DIMENSIONS
MAY VARY)

24" ON CENTER

2' - 0" TO STUDS

5' - 5" STUD WALL

BETWEEN WALLS (A) & (C)

8' - 0" PLATFORM WIDTH

TUFTEX CORRUGATED
ROOFING

1x6 OR 2x6 FASCIA
BOARD FOR FINISH

WALL (A)

2x6 FLOOR
BOARDS

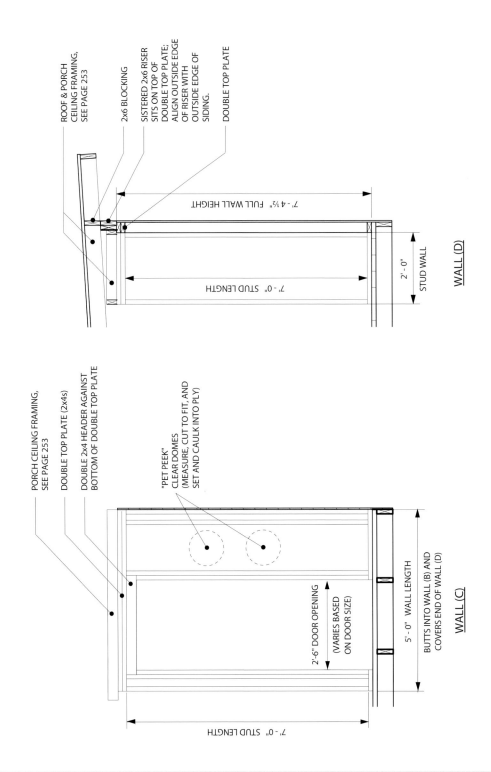

WALL (D)

ROOF & PORCH CEILING FRAMING, SEE PAGE 253

2x6 BLOCKING

SISTERED 2x6 RISER SITS ON TOP OF DOUBLE TOP PLATE; ALIGN OUTSIDE EDGE OF RISER WITH OUTSIDE EDGE OF SIDING.

DOUBLE TOP PLATE

7' - 4½" FULL WALL HEIGHT

7' - 0" STUD LENGTH

2' - 0" STUD WALL

WALL (C)

PORCH CEILING FRAMING, SEE PAGE 253

DOUBLE TOP PLATE (2x4s)

DOUBLE 2x4 HEADER AGAINST BOTTOM OF DOUBLE TOP PLATE

"PET PEEK" CLEAR DOMES (MEASURE, CUT TO FIT, AND SET AND CAULK INTO PLY)

2' - 6" DOOR OPENING (VARIES BASED ON DOOR SIZE)

5' - 0" WALL LENGTH BUTTS INTO WALL (B) AND COVERS END OF WALL (D)

7' - 0" STUD LENGTH

WALL (E) FRAMING (VIEW FROM INSIDE)

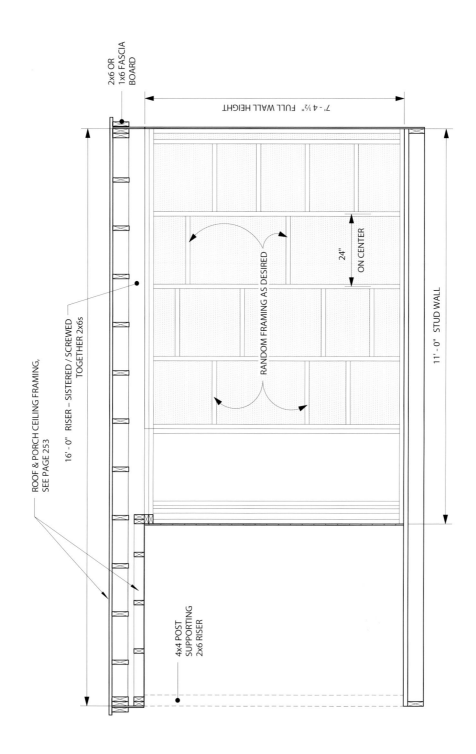

2x6 OR 1x6 FASCIA BOARD

7' - 4 ½" FULL WALL HEIGHT

24" ON CENTER

RANDOM FRAMING AS DESIRED

11' - 0" STUD WALL

ROOF & PORCH CEILING FRAMING, SEE PAGE 253

16' - 0" RISER – SISTERED / SCREWED TOGETHER 2x6s

4x4 POST SUPPORTING 2x6 RISER

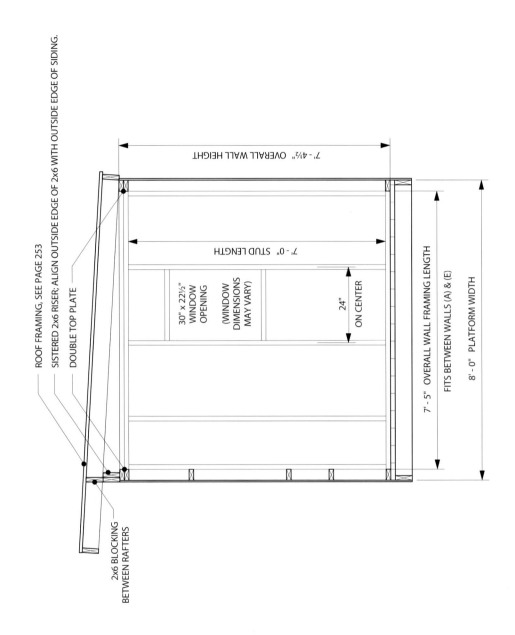

ROOF FRAMING, SEE PAGE 253

SISTERED 2x6 RISER; ALIGN OUTSIDE EDGE OF 2x6 WITH OUTSIDE EDGE OF SIDING.

DOUBLE TOP PLATE

2x6 BLOCKING
BETWEEN RAFTERS

7' - 4½" OVERALL WALL HEIGHT

7' - 0" STUD LENGTH

30" x 22½"
WINDOW
OPENING

(WINDOW
DIMENSIONS
MAY VARY)

24"

ON CENTER

7' - 5" OVERALL WALL FRAMING LENGTH

FITS BETWEEN WALLS (A) & (E)

8' - 0" PLATFORM WIDTH

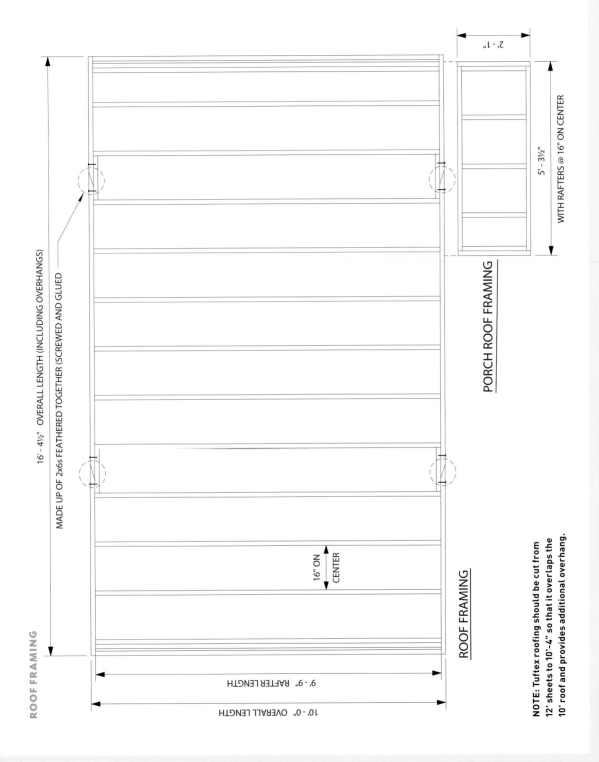

ROOF FRAMING

16' - 4½" OVERALL LENGTH (INCLUDING OVERHANGS)

MADE UP OF 2x6s FEATHERED TOGETHER (SCREWED AND GLUED)

16" ON CENTER

ROOF FRAMING

9' - 9" RAFTER LENGTH

10' - 0" OVERALL LENGTH

2' - 1"

5' - 3½"

WITH RAFTERS @ 16" ON CENTER

PORCH ROOF FRAMING

NOTE: Tuftex roofing should be cut from 12' sheets to 10'-4" so that it overlaps the 10' roof and provides additional overhang.

A Word (or a thousand) of Thanks

IT'S BEEN A CRAZY JOURNEY, and I've met many creative, kind, and supportive people, some of whom I now consider good friends — and all through the tiny house scene, which is a bit of a "trip." Not to thank the appropriate people would just be wrong. I wear my influences on my sleeve . . .

MY WIFE, LIZ — an ultra-tolerant, loving, and supportive woman. I'm beyond lucky to have her. Liz, thanks for not killing me for the messes, paperwork, and mountains of salvaged lumber around the yard! She is more responsible for what you've seen from me in more ways than you will know.

DUSTIN, MY BROTHER — my right-hand man, a best friend. I'm lucky to have shared so many construction adventures with him, from Fargo to Sydney and everywhere in between.

STEVEN HARRELL — an all-around nut and good friend who has helped spread the word many times when it comes to my work. Steven runs Tiny House Listings online and is one of the funnier dudes I know. We've had some great times traveling, filming, building, plotting, and hangin'!

KENT GRISWOLD KENT — Kent (a.k.a. "K-Grizz") is one of the O.G.s of the scene. Without his blog work, this scene would not be what it is, or might not be a scene at all. While new waves of young, green, new-jack bloggers pop up everywhere (not a bad thing), it's the-behind-the-scenes guys like Kent who have made this happen. Recognize!

JAY SHAFER — (look the man up) is another one who doesn't get acknowledged enough by the newer generation of tiny house fans.

ALEX PINO — a.k.a. "The Cuban Connection" or "A-bomb," as I call him. He's a mega-blogger (Tiny House Talk) who has also helped me out nonstop. A good dude, too.

LLOYD KAHN — they don't make 'em any cooler than this guy. His books through Shelter Publications are among the best and have inspired me on more than one occasion.

MY PARENTS (Glenn and Sigrid Diedricksen) — two incredibly cool, open-minded, creative, and fun people who gave me an amazing upbringing. They were also very tolerant of the six thousand or so forts I built in the backyard growing up in Madison, Connecticut.

ANDREW "SWEET TEA" ODOM (a.k.a. "Beardy") — for his support and humor, and for being a reciprocating ear and soundboard for out-there ideas.

SEAN CAREY — a former student in my workshop, now a freelance architect-extraordinaire. A special McMansion-sized thanks for lending his hand toward making my chicken-scratch drawings and late-night e-mail descriptions a reality in the form of the CAFAM framing plans (page 240).

A BIG THANKS ALSO TO Joe Everson of Tennessee Tiny Homes; Michael Janzen (another online pioneer with Tiny House Design); Mike Bedsole of Tiny House Chattanooga; Domenic Mangano of the Jamaica Cottage Shop in Vermont; Joshua and Shelley Engberg from Tiny House Basics; and BTR, a.k.a. "Roy St. Clair," a very helpful individual and friend.

ALSO, SHOUTS TO MY ROAD TEAM — Marty "Baccardi" Skrelunas, "Shippey" (Jim Shippey), and Palo "Bump" Coleman — for the help, good times, and long-winded tales (most of them about bamboo, Germany, or obscure industrial bands).

Left to right: Steven Harrell of TinyHouseListings.com, Dustin Diedricksen, and Derek "Deek" Diedricksen

METRIC CONVERSIONS

US	METRIC
⅛ inch	3.2 mm
¼ inch	6.35 mm
⅜ inch	9.5 mm
½ inch	1.27 cm
⅝ inch	1.59 cm
¾ inch	1.91 cm
⅞ inch	2.22 cm
1 inch	2.54 cm

TO CONVERT	TO	MULTIPLY
inches	millimeters	inches by 25.4
inches	centimeters	inches by 2.54
inches	meters	inches by 0.0254
feet	meters	feet by 0.3048

Build (on) Your Dreams with More Books from Storey

BY DEREK "DEEK" DIEDRICKSEN

Get inspired with this quirky collection of creative cabins, forts, studios, and other tiny getaways. The floor plans, building guidelines, and tips on using recycled materials will get you started constructing your dream shelter.

BY WILL HOLMAN

Join the explosion of interest in handcrafting furnishings from found and sustainable materials. These 31 projects offer step-by-step instructions for making stylish, functional, and economical tables, chairs, lamps, and more out of reclaimed paper, wood, plastic, and metal.

BY GERALD ROWAN

Simple living in 1,000 square feet or less! With 62 design interpretations for every taste, this fully illustrated guide will inspire your dream cabin. These innovative floor plans are flexible, with modular elements to mix and match.

BY GERALD ROWAN

Live comfortably in 1,400 square feet or less with these 50 innovative floor plans. Whether you're building from scratch or retrofitting, use these efficient and creative layouts to design an efficient house that has everything you need.

Join the conversation. Share your experience with this book, learn more about Storey Publishing's authors, and read original essays and book excerpts at storey.com.
Look for our books wherever quality books are sold or call 800-441-5700.